CHARLES LONG

LIFE AFTER THE CITY

A HARROWSMITH GUIDE TO RURAL LIVING

CAMDEN HOUSE

For Mary Smale

CAMDEN
◆HOUSE◆

PUBLISHING

Canadian Cataloguing in Publication Data

Long, Charles
    Life after the city

ISBN 0-920656-14-5

1. Country life.   2. Urban-rural migration.
I. Title.

S521.L66 1989   307.7'2   C89-093835-0

Trade distribution by
Firefly Books
250 Sparks Avenue
Willowdale, Ontario
Canada M2H 2S4

Printed in Canada for
Camden House Publishing
(a division of Telemedia Publishing Inc.)
7 Queen Victoria Road
Camden East, Ontario
K0K 1J0

Design by
Andrew McLachlan

Cover illustration
by Stephen Quinlan

Printed and bound in Canada by
D.W. Friesen & Sons
Altona, Manitoba

CONTENTS

▼▼▼▼▼

Acknowledgements

My thanks to Elizabeth Long for help with the research and for her quiet counsel along the way.

Thanks, too, to all those friends and neighbours whose stories fill these pages. I've changed a few details for privacy's sake, and a few things I probably got wrong, but if some passage sounds familiar, yes, it's probably you. Without you, this book (and this life) would be poorer.

Finally, I am indebted to my publisher Frank Edwards, who conceived this project, and to the staff at Camden House who laboured to bring it forth — designer Andrew McLachlan, assistant editor Charlotte DuChene, copy editors Catherine De Lury and Judith Knopp Brown and typographer Patricia Denard-Hinch.

PROLOGUE

There is nothing dumber than a chicken. Nothing. We have nine middle-aged hens right now. They average about six eggs a day. So we keep six nest boxes for them. The boxes are whitewashed and lined with fluffy, dry grass. There's a slatted walkway along the front, so they can strut up and down to find a vacant box whenever the urge strikes. Short of installing a hot tub, there's little we could do to make the old dears more comfy.

What's so dumb about them? They all try to crawl into the same box at the same time. Every day. This morning, I found three hens on the same nest, one on top of the next, with three broken eggs under the half-dead hen at the bottom. The other five nests were empty.

It isn't that one of the boxes is any better than the rest. They're all exactly the same. Indeed, the daily pileup changes boxes almost every day. The first hen sits on any old nest at random, then all the rest start to squeeze in with her. They don't really enjoy it. They squawk and bicker and peck one another's feathers out when it gets too crowded. But they're just too damned dumb to notice that the box next door is just as nice and considerably more comfortable. Or maybe they notice and then decide that if the empty boxes were habitable, they wouldn't be empty.

I was thinking about that this morning when I read that 76 percent of us live in cities.

FREE WILL

This is a book about deciding where to live. About choices. It is, in part, about the choice between city and country living. But more than that, it's about the very fact that the choice exists. It's a look ahead. A look at the possibilities just opened to many, and soon to be opened to many more. Possibilities to rearrange some of the elements of life into a more satisfying order.

There are some broad reasons a former necessity has become a choice: the dispersal of industry and jobs away from city centres and the technical revolution that has decentralized access to information, the economy and even the culture. The sum of these changes is the end of rural isolation as we once knew it. More about that later.

Here, in the beginning, let's take a peek at a few of the narrower, more personal reasons we live where we do. Historically, we lived wherever we happened to be born. Or in times of want, we moved wherever food might be found. Not much free will in that. In more recent times, we moved where careers dictated or where spouses' careers dictated. And often, like the chickens, we ended up in uncomfortable places for no good reason at all.

If that sounds too sweeping, if the "we" does not include you, forgive me. That generalization, like others that follow, comes out of my own experience. You'll find statistics in these pages and occasional references to experts read and interviewed in order to flesh out ideas. But most of the arguments come from the lives of the people and places I know best. Your own experience may be different. I hope so. But those differences nevertheless leave us in a bit of an editorial pickle. What kind of shape should these ideas take? A bureaucrat would qualify every conclusion with enough loopholes and equivocal clauses to cover every possible exception. An academic would use lots of quotes from fellow academics and pages of data to prove statistically that when we differ, I'm right and you're wrong – overwhelming the reader with numbers and insider jargon.

Fortunately, there's a third editorial choice – admit frankly that this is neither a thesis nor a political statement but a personal view of the world. Let's not pretend it's science and then lose sight of the important stuff in a lot of silly arguments over definitions and methods.

If we disagree, let's blame it on different preferences or different perspectives on the world. If I fail to persuade urban readers that the city has its limits, then that's fine too. For I would be the first to regret any mass migration to the country. At the very best, I hope that these pages will at least prick a few too comfortable myths about urban and rural lives. And I hope that they spark a closer look at why you live where you do and what the alternatives might be.

But I digress. We were talking about how "we" ended up in unlikely places for no good reason, and I paused for the protests of those who would exempt themselves from such generalizations. Fine. Let's be specific. I drifted along like the chickens, riding the tides of opportunity or impulse and believing, like Candide, that in this best of all possible worlds, things could not be otherwise. If Gallup or the academics had ever bothered to ask, I could have given lots of sensible reasons for where I was and what I was doing at any given time. And most of the reasons, in hindsight, were so much codswallop.

The truth is always sillier than the rationalizations. The truth is that I once emigrated from the United States to Australia because that was as far from Cleveland as I could get on the proceeds from my only asset, a red Harley-Davidson motorcycle with balky gears and a leaky gas tank. And we (my wife Liz and I) finally settled on a hundred acres of trees and rocks in eastern Ontario because we walked across the land in May, when trilliums covered the forest floor and dazzled us with a vision of how beautiful it could be. Our personal geography has never been more scientific than that.

If we did finally get it right on the last move, almost 15 years ago, it's at least partly due to the wisdom of trial and error. Between us, we've settled in four different countries, half a dozen cities and as many rural places. It's hard not to get it right after that many tries. And it's hard, admittedly, to make a choice when every place has its attractions. I have come to prefer country living, although I still love

7

cities and still enjoy them in ways that don't require living inside their limits. If that's a contradiction, I insist on leaving it unresolved.

So, trial and error, plus two other realizations, brought us here. The first is that you don't have to live in a place to enjoy it. In my eyes, Venice is the most charming city in Europe, but those who live there year-round must worry about rising tides, eroding foundations, hordes of tourists and the stench of the canals in summer. The second realization, the one that took longest to see, is that Utopia does not exist. A tropical climate includes tropical insects. A mountain view is at the end of a mountain road. Urban services come with a crowd. And nature's charms are nowhere on the subway line. Sooner or later, most of us have to settle down someplace, anyplace, and live our lives. The best we can do is choose one of the pleasant places and keep most of the things we love within reach.

These are the personal reasons people live where they do. Family, jobs and plain old likes and dislikes are central parts of the equation, as are chance and happenstance, and all of that would appear to make it futile to apply science to such a question. Social science can't pretend to know anything about the future, which is all that really matters when you're deciding something so basic as where to live. Sociologists and economists can tell you what happened last year or what happened to a sample of people in the last census year. But they cannot tell you whether those people are happy with what they've done or describe the quality of the things that have happened. I make no apology for writing from human experience and not from sociological data. These are subjective questions. My only nod in the direction of objectivity is to announce my rural bias at the beginning and let the reader be warned.

CITY LIMITS

▼▼▼▼▼

Villagers and country people regard the city with the same quiet superiority that Canadians feel toward the United States and that Americans feel toward Europe. It is, for the most part, a kindly sort of superiority, not brash and smug but polite and usually unspoken. It arises from the simple fact that rural dwellers can enjoy the best things cities have to offer . . . without the inconvenience of actually living there.

The people of St. Marys or Tincap, Ontario, go to Toronto to cheer Blue Jays baseball, to shop at the Eaton Centre, to hear the symphony and to enjoy the theatre. They have a good time and then go home again, shaking their heads at the urbanites left behind to fight the daily 5 o'clock rush on the parkway and to pay their crushing mortgages.

Is that so different from the Canadians who enjoy Hollywood films and Florida beaches or go to New York for Broadway musicals? They might have a wonderful time, but they still wouldn't dream of living year-round with the violence, the litter and the redneck politics that some of us have grown to associate with America.

Is that so different from Americans in Europe savouring the relics of the past while scorning the hidebound bureaucracies that have kept the relics unchanged? A nice-place-to-visit-but-I-wouldn't-want-to-live-there feeling.

Of course, the feeling works both ways. City folks visit the country for clean lakes and cottages and then wonder how the locals manage to live there through the winter. Americans come to Canada and then go home relieved that they, at least, don't have to live with high Canadian prices and metric road signs. And Europeans gawk at the Grand Canyon and muse about how much more livable the United States might be with decent public transportation.

Then we all go home from wherever we've been and feel better about where we live. In Dallas and Paris and Smooth Rock Falls, we sit down to watch American films with Canadian locations on Japanese television sets, cozy up in Hong Kong slippers, keep warm with Venezuelan oil, sip a little French burgundy or munch a Georgian peanut and wonder how the others manage to live in less blessed places.

Maybe it's just as well that we can all feel a little bit self-satisfied about the places where we live. Otherwise, we might all be eaten alive with envy. Or, we might wander forever in search of the best of all possible worlds, so busy looking for Utopia that we never actually get down to tending our own gardens. It may be true that where we live matters less than what we make of it. And it is certainly true that if we are not wholly mobile, then the rest of the world is—

McDonald's and Mitsubishi will come to us no matter where we are.

But there is a risk in feeling even a little bit smug. The risk is that we tie ourselves to places that change. And if we don't examine those places from time to time and our reasons for being there, we end up in ruts that might not be quite so rewarding as we imagine them.

Three-quarters of Americans live in cities, and yet a 1986 Gallup poll tells us that half of American adults would really rather live in the country. What keeps them in the city, discontent and yearning for something else and yet obscuring their discontent with pride of place and bumper stickers that say "I heart New York"? Are we all a little bit schizophrenic? Maybe so.

Take Toronto. Its denizens call it the most livable city in North America. And it is very nice: much safer than nearby Detroit, prettier than Pittsburgh, easier for commuters than New York. Torontonians have a right to be a little bit smug, which is why I was feeling uneasy as the only out-of-towner at a recent summer barbecue in the comfortable suburbs of that city.

It was akin to being the only Blue Jays fan in Yankee Stadium. The hundred or so guests were mostly on the youngish side of middle age, mostly upscale enough to compare winter vacations and all convinced that Copernicus would have had the sun turn around Toronto, if only he had known. Among the most ardent boosters were the recent arrivals: an Irishman with a new development house cheering on the housing boom, a Californian touting the merits of the GO Train, and a goodly sample of Englishmen weighing the odds on the local baseball team.

There's more, but the main point is the house, the star of the afternoon. Everybody raved about what a wonderful place it was. Not the actual building. That was nice enough, but it wasn't the house, it was the site that sent the assemblage into raptures.

"There are so many trees!" (This said with a sweep of the arm to the leafy horizon a hundred feet away.)

"You can barely see the highway!"

" . . . and when the leaves are out and the wind is blowing the other way, that traffic noise is just a hum."

" . . . and when those baby trees along the lot line grow, you won't be able to see that dirt pile from the neighbour's pool."

Again and again, we remarked on these charms and inevitably summed them up by saying, "It's almost like living in the country!" The compliments were sincere, but we missed the irony that should have been plain to a country person. Think about it. The luckiest people, in the most livable city, save their highest praise for a house whose greatest virtue is pretending not to be in the city. "Like living in the country!" The fact is, there are lots of places in the real country where it's not "almost" but just exactly like living in the country: trees, ravines, and you certainly can't see the neighbour's dirt pile or hear the highway – even with all the leaves off the trees – and at about one-fifth of the cost.

We'll come back to the real cost of places like this one later. For now, let's pry just a little bit deeper into the lives of the hosts. Why do they live here (besides the fact that it's almost like being in the country)?

It's convenient, they could say. Less than an hour to their downtown offices. (The average rural person spends half that time getting to work.)

There's more money in Toronto, they could say. She works in a bank that has identical branches in every hamlet from Armstrong, British Columbia, to Tickle Cove, Newfoundland. He has his own company, doing business all over the continent. The geographic centre of his trade is probably somewhere in Minnesota.

It's not the nightlife. He plays basketball at the YMCA (20 miles away) and makes wine (in the basement). They enjoy films but have only been to one this year. It's easier to pick up a video and avoid the trek downtown.

That's part of the contented half of the urban populace. The other half, the half that would rather be living in the real country, is no less enmeshed in the little deceptions that keep us where we are.

All of us – bumper-sticker urbophiles, city gardeners, job-trapped dreamers, back-to-the-landers and never-left-the-landers – all of us get stuck in mental ruts, taking our image of what life must be like elsewhere from outdated clichés. The fact is that reality has changed much faster than has our vision of it. It isn't even fair to use the simple words like "urban" and "rural," "country" and "city." Not without some qualification. The new reality isn't that simple. The clear distinctions between the two places have blurred. The images remain, but the realities behind them have changed.

The truth is more complex. The truth is that while 25 percent of us do live outside the cities, only 4 percent of us live on farms. And yet, in the image business, "rural" is a near synonym for "farm."

When government wants a rural view, they ask the opinion of farm organizations. Nothing could be less representative. The truth is that

12

the average rural dweller wouldn't know one end of a plough from another and the average urbanite does not get mugged on the way to work. The truth is that clean water may be as big a problem in the pristine countryside as it is in the city. The truth is that homicide may be as common in the village as it is in some big bad cities. The truth is that jobs may be easier to find in some small towns than in big ones. The truth is that rural people may exercise more cultural options than their urban cousins. The truth is that rapid inflation of urban housing prices may make paper riches and pauper lives for their owners. The truth is that rural homeowners may have more disposable income than their urban counterparts. The truth is that the city may not be the focus of riches and convenience that it imagines itself to be. And moving to the country may be a little more complicated than the simple urge to watch things grow.

Within that web of stereotypes and rapidly changing truths, we must be careful with simple terms like "rural" and "urban." If we were bureaucrats or academics, we might invent new words to describe the new realities. We might talk about dispersed urban values in nonagricultural low-density environments, countrified cities or "rurban" man. But that would only add to the confusion. Let's just stick to rural and urban and have a little understanding between ourselves that those words don't mean all the same things that they used to mean.

For most people, through most of history, where to live has not been a decision. We lived where our parents lived or wherever employment happened to take us. We chose this neighbourhood over that one. We chose a street or a house but not much more than that. We stayed in our places or went to the places where the jobs went.

Even the immigrants, those pioneers who moved across continents and seas, rarely had the luxury of choice. They left where they were because hardship or war made the old places unlivable. And they came to this place or that one because it was the only place that would take them or the only place they could reach.

Late in the 14th century, the plague depopulated Europe and revolutionized the way most people lived and worked. The serfs, for as long as any of them could remember, had been bound from birth to death to a particular lord and his land. Then, in the space of a few years, much of the once productive land was emptied. The lord who "owned" it might be dead. Certainly many of those who had worked the fields were dead. Those who survived were still bound in place, expected to continue paying rent and donating labour to the old lord or his heirs.

13

From wherever they toiled, they could see neighbouring land abandoned, where the fields went untilled from lack of hands, where crops might belong to whoever grew them.

Not surprisingly, some of those surviving serfs said "to hell with this" and moved onto lands where rents were smaller or never collected. They took it upon themselves to decide where to live.

What is surprising is that more of them didn't chuck the old place for a better life down the road. Church and landowners did their best to hold the toilers in their inherited places. But the clout of the establishment had been too crippled by the plague to keep all of them down on the farm for long.

It was plague, then open land and opportunity that helped to break the back of feudalism and set free a part of the once submissive masses.

The modern parallel to that upheaval might be the revolution in industrial patterns that has emptied North American factories and much of the old industrial heart of the continent. Freed from the serfdom of the assembly line, some workers have fought to stay in their old ruts and, hand in hand with the corporations, have demanded that governments pump more investment into dying industries in last-gasp efforts to keep them afloat. Others, seeing opportunity, have moved down the road to the new industries.

It was little different when feudalism died. Some stayed on with the old masters or quickly found new ones. Others moved on to new opportunities. They became the free yeomen, the mercenary soldiers, the artisans and city folk that peopled the new Europe.

The cities grew and then grew even more as steam began to drive the first industrial revolution. The cities coalesced around the ports, roads and rivers that brought trade goods together. The factories that both used and produced trade goods grew in the cities. The industrial appetite for labour attracted new waves of people from the countryside. The swelling mass fed on itself. Mass production needed ready pools of labour, and the labourers became the market for what the factories produced.

In that age, society assumed that the common man's purpose was to work. He had little choice but to live above the shop or within a short walk of the factory gate. Rows of worker housing grew around the mills. Almost all the waking day was for work. Even if there had been suburbs and cars, there would not have been time enough to commute. There was barely time enough in the day to eat, sleep and create replacements.

Like any tide, the rush from country to city created its own counterforce. The very crush at the centre made land and transportation dear. By the time trucks and airplanes had freed industry from its former dependence on canals, railroads and other fixed lines, few industries could afford to be downtown. They began to move out beyond the city limits.

At the same time, the car freed the workers from their dependence on the factory house. It was no longer necessary to sleep above the shop. Just as it had once ceased to be necessary to stay on the old feudal estate.

The cities, obviously, didn't empty. Shopping and office blocks filled the spaces that the factories had vacated. The rail yards and warehouses of 50 years ago became the malls and condos of today. Urban slum became urban chic and attracted a new kind of worker. Now, while the latter-day lemmings still rush in to be at the centre of things, the economy that feeds the core has begun to move and change again.

The nut of the thing is that we no longer need to be places anymore. Just as the factories no longer needed to be right on the railway line after the invention of the truck, white-collar workers no longer need to sit in the same room to process insurance claims, answer telephones, analyze stocks, sell widgets, send invoices, plan, invent or tell others what to do.

It's not that cities have become unlivable, although some have. It's just that cities are becoming unnecessary.

When smokestack factories realized that they no longer needed to occupy the most congested and expensive land in the city, they moved. When the new urban industries reach that conclusion, they, too, will move. Some have already begun. The fast-growing, high-tech leaders of the pack in the new information economy haven't sprouted in the centres of cities. They're suburban, even rural.

More importantly, some workers have reached the same conclusion and have discovered ways to earn a living in this newly reordered world. Ways that no longer require them to live in the city. They might still want to live in the city. But a former necessity has become a choice.

Shorter working hours and the automobile put an end to the necessity, if not the practice, of living by the job. We could sleep in one suburb and shop in another, work downtown and spend weekends in the country. But where, in that mobile sprawl, do we actually "live"? Is the focus where we get the mail? Is it where we sleep? Where we work? Where we enjoy life most? The truth of the matter is that life has lost much of the centre that too much work once provided.

Even the fast-fading eight-hour day fills less than a fifth of our total time. The geographic focus of the workplace is gone. Not only do we have the time and the mobility to spread our lives more widely, but the workplace itself has scattered.

Family life decentralizes us even more. If you're a family, the odds say that you're a two-income family. If you're an urban family, you almost have to be a two-income family, and the chances are that you drive off in two directions to earn those two incomes. Older children develop their own interests and scatter to all other points, usually needing a ride.

The problem is that while the choices have expanded, so have the distances between them. Blame the automobile or the sheer size of cities. Whatever the reason, the fact is that we spend a lot more time moving around. Even those who still live over the shop or beside the office have to accept that the supermarket has moved to a suburban mall, cinemas someplace else, the parks and schools in another direction. And soon, the office itself will move to cheaper land out of town.

The scattering of the old industrial core has led to a new phenomenon called "reverse commuting." It describes those who live downtown and commute to jobs in the suburbs. This would seem to be a short-lived trend, doomed to die the moment these workers figure out that it's no more convenient to commute in reverse than it was to commute in forward and that it is more costly to pay the downtown prices which their employers were wise enough to flee.

So why, in all this entropic scattering of life's activities, do some still feel bound to nest within an easy drive of the old industrial core? Or within some traditional range of their partner's job? The fact is that every member of the family spends a large part of every day commuting to a variety of activities. And the problem doesn't disappear with clever home buying. You can sleep right on the office floor and still have to fight your way to the mall for groceries or to the countryside for a change of scene. And everyone else in the family will still be commuting to their jobs and classes.

If transportation were the only measure, the rational way to decide where to live would be to add up all the trips and find the focus at the epicentre of the entire web, equidistant from school, choir, scouts, cottage, beach, shops and the workplace.

Even that would not be easy. Modern cities have grown so large that they've begun to grow together. Where is the focus of the Eastern Seaboard? Of the Great Lakes Basin? The overlapping sprawl undermines the primary advantage of the city – concentration. There cannot be one centre, one downtown for the entire world. There are many centres, and as they grow together, it begins to matter less and less where one sleeps. If you work in a large organization that operates throughout a wide cluster of merging cities, finding one centre may be impossible. My little village of Rideau Ferry is as central to Canada as Toronto is. And the Torontonian is much farther removed from Montreal and New York than I am.

The ancient symbol for "city" was a cross within a circle, the intersection of paths within the city wall. The difference today is that there are many more paths that crisscross in other places and other dimensions, and the walls, of course, are gone.

If we were to invent a modern hieroglyphic for the city, it would have to be a matrix, not a single intersection. A matrix, perhaps, of dotted lines, in three dimensions, a web that is no longer physical, no longer linear, no longer confined to one place within the walls.

The changes, and the failure to see them, remind me of those little, tiny dots on the map in the middle of Kansas or Iowa or wherever the places are that advertise themselves as the exact geographic centre of the United States or North America or whatever. The joke is that only the people who live there know or care. The centre has not held. And then there was my friend Cyril from Tipperary, who always insisted that only the Irish spoke a pure English, undiluted by any accent. He went red in the face trying to convince a roomful of Scots, Londoners, Americans, Canadians and Australians that their speech was sullied with provincialisms. The joke was that nobody but Cyril cared, so long as we could all be understood. The centre had not held, and Cyril was the last to know.

And the people who mortgage two careers to squeeze themselves into a city that they imagine to be the centre of something might also be the last to know that the rest of the world doesn't care. Call it urban sprawl, social entropy, the global village or a globe of villages. It doesn't matter. We'll leave that to the social theorists. They can argue with Cyril about where the centre of the world is.

Our purpose here is not to spot the trends or to persuade anybody to move anywhere. Our purpose is to dispel some outdated myths about town and country and to suggest some alternatives to those who feel trapped by the costs and occasional unpleasantness of trying to live "in the centre."

17

If we were to confine ourselves to the statistical argument, we would have to say that in North America, the people trend is indeed toward living in the "centre." Statistically, the cities are growing faster than small towns and rural places, but anything the statistics could say about small places would have to be qualified by the fact that each little place is very different from other little places. And big numbers obscure these small distinctions.

Some little places are successful and some aren't. If small towns in the Annapolis and Okanagan valleys, Colorado and Nevada are showing a new vibrancy, it must also be said that rural Saskatchewan is hanging on by its toenails, that Gatineau mill towns are still ugly and that Duck Run, Ohio, has been duller than ditch water since Leonard Sly left town to become Roy Rogers a half-century ago.

A big city, like a supermarket, is almost certain to have at least one of everything—a transportation system, restaurants, sports, theatre, and so on. By contrast, the small town may have good sports facilities and few dining spots. The next small town may have lively cafés but no sporting life to speak of. That diversity can make choosing a place in the country much more difficult than choosing a city. There is more to be learned, and there are more differences to weigh.

One of the failings of the old back-to-the-land movement was its uncritical belief in all things rural. Its proponents argued that outside the city limits, the world was somehow purer. It wasn't. Rural people can be as stunted and grasping as city people. And rural people can be as smart and sophisticated as city people. Some back-to-the-landers were disillusioned. And, as we shall see, some figured out that the real world isn't so easily boxed into categories of good and evil.

PAPER RICHES, PAUPER LIVES

▼▼▼▼▼

There are some times in the life of the world when it pays to be going the other way, to step out of the parade and march in the opposite direction – lemmings come to mind, or the rush to buy stocks in the summer of '87. This may be one of those times. When most of the world is squeezing itself into giant cities, some of us wrong-way lemmings ask why.

Not that we're such a tiny voice. If polls show that fully half of urban America would really rather live in the country, that yearning must be nearer 100 percent at rush hour on any expressway or bus.

In some cities, at some times, we might be able to blame the place itself for such high levels of dissatisfaction. Some are certainly too ugly, too dirty or too brutish ever to inspire much civic satisfaction. Many aren't. Vancouver has its perfect setting. Paris has its boulevards.

Why, then, is there such a high level of dissatisfaction? Even in the nice cities? My guess is that there's a streak of nature in all of us. Not really the call of the wild – there's little enough of that left anywhere. But a dream of peace and security, one place with sufficient privacy and space to be ourselves without thinking about what others might say or do. As kids, we made a treehouse in the woods, where no adults could come. My son makes forts, with stone redoubts and treetop lookouts. The streak runs deep. Adults, even the hard-core urban kind, retreat to a cottage by the lake, to the boat, to a hunt camp or to one place in their lives where they can be raucous or quiet, naked or absurd, silly and lazy or nothing at all, and nobody makes demands. There's a rose-covered cottage inside every soul; but rarely does it come to light in the city.

The surprising thing is that those deep yearnings seldom translate into action. It may be that the yearning is so often submerged under a cold, wet blanket of misconceptions and unanswered questions. What is country life really like? Could I make a living there? Could I afford to make such a move? Could I really live without the city goodies? And could I afford to come back if country life palls?

The uncertainty is usually enough to kill the urge. And if that doesn't do it, a full appraisal of all the city's admitted seductions will take the steam out of most frustrations. Finally, for some, there's that big rusty anchor of real estate to keep us from drifting far.

Be it ever so humble, the house has been growing in value at a mind-boggling rate over the past few years. The hot market jacked up the value of the average Canadian house by almost $24,000 from April 1986 to April 1987, from under $91,000 to $114,500. And that was an average. The windfall "profit" was even larger in the bigger cities. Toronto homeowners saw their investments soar by almost 50 percent in the same period, from $133,000 to more than $200,000 – an average gain of $67,000! Had you moved from Toronto to the country in the year before, you would have missed those spectacular gains. The market cooled off a bit in the year that followed. By April 1988, a three-bedroom Toronto house was up by only about 15 percent. That's still not a bad investment. It's even better when you consider the leverage that a mortgage gives.

Now, if numbers like that leave a little smile on your face, enough to stifle any rural urges, look just a little closer at the gains. First, consider the fact that every penny of that "profit" is plain old nasty inflation. The lot hasn't grown any bigger, the house hasn't improved itself. That $67,000 came from the ether. Nothing was made or grown to produce it, nothing was sold, no service rendered. It was paper profit. It was inflation.

That kind of inflation, however, doesn't have many negative feelings about it, if you happen to be on the receiving end.

If you're smiling over housing prices, you can imagine how happy the Saudis were when OPEC put oil prices through the ceiling. Same old barrel of oil, same old buyers, but lots and lots of new money. Same old house, same old city, but $67,000 of brand-new paper riches. If the comparison rankles, ask any young couple who have yet to buy their first house, who have been saving faithfully for that first down payment and watched the price go up faster than they can possibly save. To buy that $200,000 Toronto house, our young couples have to come up with a $50,000 down payment and almost $19,000 a year for mortgage and taxes. Even with an average family income of $48,675, buyers would still be turned down by 9 out of 10 lending institutions. That's what inflation means.

But if you already own your own home, housing inflation puts a smile on your face and a bounce in your step. You might hesitate even to consider a move: If I sell out now, I'll miss next year's gains. If I sell out now, I'll never be able to buy back in later. If there were a fast train to hell and the passengers were paid a thousand dollars a mile to stay on, the question would be the same: How long can I stay on before it's too late?

With all those brakes on the dream of the rose-covered cottage, is it any wonder that small towns and rural places have grown slowly and steadily while many big cities have boomed? The logic of money says, "Stay on as long as you can." Or does it?

Just for the sake of argument, extend the stay-put logic to some other red-hot real estate market. To Tokyo, for example, or Mexico City. There's even more growth pressure there and more inflation than in Toronto. Mexican homeowners rode the crest of a 103 percent inflation rate in the year Toronto housing went up a paltry 50 percent. Between 1985 and 1988, the cost of a detached house with three bedrooms and 2½ bathrooms in a good Mexico City neighbourhood more than quadrupled in value, from approximately 20 million pesos to 90 million. If a hot housing market is all that keeps you in the city, you may be in the wrong city. If you had put your $50,000 down payment into Mexico City, you might have done much better than in Toronto. The logic of inflation would still be saying, "If we sell out and leave Mexico City now, we'll miss out on next year's gains, and if we sell now, we might never be able to buy back in later."

But wait. Mexico City? Why would we want to live in Mexico City? Isn't it so polluted that birds drop dead from the sky? So choked with its 18 million that nothing really works very well? Maybe. But some of the people who live there must like it. Certainly those who made a bundle on the red-hot housing market would be reluctant to move anywhere else. They're afraid that they'll miss out on next year's profits if they sell out now. And they're afraid that if they change their minds, they may never be able to afford to get back on that fast train to riches.

That's the way it goes. If the main reason for staying in Toronto or Buffalo or Boston is the simple fear of getting off the gravy train too soon, take heart. The people in small towns and rural places feel much the same way about Toronto as you feel about Mexico City. It might be a nice place to visit, but live there? Just to make paper profits on inflation?

For the homeowner, the pressure to stay with the crowd is enormous. The leverage from a mortgage distorts the apparent advantage even more. Consider our Toronto home buyer who paid $133,000 in 1986 for a house that would sell for $200,000 the following year. If he had paid the $133,000 in cash, inflation would have given him a one-year paper profit of 50 percent. If, on the other hand, he had bought the house with a normal down payment of $33,000 and a $100,000 mortgage, his gross profit on a 1987 resale would be the same, $67,000. But the rate of return on the smaller down payment invested would be much greater. If the interest on the mortgage had cost him $10,000, the net return would be $57,000 on an investment of $43,000 for a handsome one-year profit of 133 percent!

Is it any wonder that homeowners – no matter how unhappy or heavily mortgaged – would want to hang on for one more mile?

WHAT'S THE CATCH?

There's a catch in all that Midas stuff, however. The catch is that the only way to turn paper profit into real profit is to sell, to get off the train. When you sell, you will still need a place to live. And if you still want to live in Toronto, you'll have to spend the same $200,000 you just made in order to buy another average house.

In fact, you will have to spend more than that. The transaction fees (surveys, mortgage fees, lawyers and real estate commissions) will eat up thousands more.

The catch is that if you want to turn paper profit into real profit, you will have to sell and leave the city. There are a couple of end runs you could try, but they, too, have their flaws. You could, for example, borrow more against the inflated equity or sell and move to a cheaper house within the city.

Borrowing against inflated equity is a no-win game. Here's how it works. The house you paid $133,000 for is now worth $200,000. When you bought, the bank wanted a 25 percent down payment and agreed to mortgage the remaining $100,000. Now, however, the bank might be willing to lend $150,000 on the same house. That works out to the same 75 percent of the resale value of the house for collateral. Now, you could refinance the house with a new $150,000 mortgage, pay off the old $100,000 mortgage and pocket the difference of $50,000.

There are variations to a straight refinancing deal. You could take out a second mortgage (at a higher interest rate). Or you could pick from an array of "home equity" loans. These come under several names but are essentially consumer loans that use the unmortgaged house equity as collateral. Interest rates are usually higher for these loans than for mortgages and are often variable rates, liable to rise at the whim of the market.

The biggest problem with borrowing against your inflated equity is that the monthly payments move up to cover the larger debt. Our Toronto homeowner who raises his mortgage from $100,000 to $150,000 also increases his payments by an extra $400 to $500 a month. If he can't earn at least that much by investing the $50,000 someplace else, then there is little point in trying to pull cash out of the house through increased borrowing.

American homeowners are in a somewhat different position. There, mortgage interest payments are tax-deductible. On the surface, it would seem to be a good idea for Americans to borrow as much as they can against the house. There is still no point in pulling out cash unless it can be put to more profitable use, but a bigger mortgage is better than other kinds of loans (mortgage payments come out of pre-tax income, consumer loans are paid out of post-tax income). As always, however, there's a catch. First of all, mortgage interest is tax-deductible in the United States only as long as the total of all mortgages and loans on the house does not exceed what you paid for the place plus the cost of any improvements. So you can't up the mortgage very far without losing the tax advantage. And most Americans who cash in by trading down to a cheaper house will pay full tax on the profits. The exception is for those over 55, who may take up to $125,000 of home-sale profits tax-free. The general rule is that nobody has much to gain by borrowing more against the house.

Selling the house outright and buying a cheaper one does take cash out of the inflated equity without the extra borrowing costs, but the advantages are dubious. First of all, inflationary housing gains are related, all across the city. So buying a cheaper house in the same city almost inevitably means buying a less desirable house. It might be smaller, in a worse neighbourhood or farther from shops and jobs. Other than the cash (which is taxable in the United States), there aren't any compensations for trading down. Unlike moving to a cheaper town (where you might buy a bigger or better house for less money), moving to a cheaper house within the same city adds new discomforts to the old ones.

INFLATION AND INTEREST

So far, we've stuck to the short-term effects and the assumption of stable mortgage interest rates in the 10 to 11 percent range. Those who were around when mortgages went up to 20 percent will know that talking about the housing market under the assumption of a low, stable rate of interest is like deciding to walk across the Sahara on a day when one lone cloud makes it momentarily cool. Happy circumstances can change. Over the life of a 25-year mortgage or a 45-year career, conditions can be counted on to change. You can bet on it.

So, no matter what the numbers say today, let's consider what might happen to that hot housing market as interest rates change. Let's start just a few short years ago, when mortgages were 20 percent and the idea of cashing in by borrowing more against the equity would have been quite absurd.

Nobody wanted to buy a house when rates were that high. The real estate boom didn't begin until interest rates started to fall. Then, with the pent-up demand, buyers gained confidence and jumped in, and builders followed. The competition for available housing pushed the prices up much faster than the overall rate of inflation. Memories of sky-high interest rates gave new buyers an extra shot of urgency – get into the market now, before the old high rates return. Once in, homeowners watched prices continue to rise and rise and rise. With smiling faces and visions of sugar plums (or BMWs), the newly paper-rich traded up, borrowed more against the increased equity or other-wise stayed out on the end of that mortgage limb. Now what happens when interest rates – for any one of a number of reasons that may have absolutely nothing to do with the housing market – begin to rise again? First, your own mortgage will follow the market rate, no matter how safe you feel you are. Most mortgages today are fixed for periods of one to five years. If the market rate goes up, sooner or later your mortgage will follow. If your mortgage lags behind a little on the way up, it will also lag behind on the way down. If you're lucky, you'll come out even.

Secondly, the rising rate quickly puts a damper on buyer enthusiasm. Fewer new buyers can afford the monthly payments it takes to get in. Existing homeowners, who might otherwise be thinking of moving or trading up, stay put; no point in refinancing their old mort-gages for new ones at the higher rates. The hot market cools off quickly. Prices stabilize or even begin to fall. If you've just bought, just pulled out some equity or otherwise got yourself mortgaged to the hilt, you're stuck. Two careers to keep up the payments, no rising values to make you feel rich and no more buyers in the wings ready to take the thing off your hands.

Even the mortgage-free have little to feel smug about. If you own the house outright and the market goes flat, that means you have your $200,000, or whatever, locked in an investment which pays no dividends and has stopped appreciating. You're making nothing on your investment, just at the time when your mortgaged neighbour is putting his assets into savings bonds at 12 percent or guaranteed investment certificates at 15 percent. At this point in the cycle, you might wish you didn't have all your assets tied up in the house.

Okay. So you're patient. You can wait out the top of the interest curve, confident that when rates eventually fall again, the buyers will come back and the prices will heat up once more. If you're well organized and can afford to bide your time, waiting for falling interest rates works. Your equity will begin to grow again.

Then something else takes over, something even more insidious because it comes from within. As interest rates fall and prices rise, the investment starts to look good again. Why give up on a winner?

The impetus to hang on is compounded for those with the leverage of a mortgage. Let's say, for example, that interest rates fall to 10 percent, which heats up the housing market to a modest 12 percent annual price increase. Our friend with the $150,000 mortgage on his $200,000 house will, within the year, see the value of his house increase by $24,000, and he will pay $15,000 in mortgage interest. That $9,000 "profit" on his $50,000 investment means an effective rate of return of 18 percent. Now if he pulls out his equity and puts it in paper investments, he'll be trading an 18 percent return for a 10 percent return. That doesn't seem like a terribly smart move.

Well, you hang onto the house because it's such a good investment. Then rates start to rise again, the buyers disappear, and suddenly it's not such a great thing to own anymore. Then the mortgage comes due, and instead of renewing at 10 percent, they now want 16 percent, which, on those higher housing values (the inflated values you were cheering about on the other side of the cycle), is an enormous sum. On a $150,000 mortgage, a 6 percent rise creates an extra $9,000 a year in extra interest charges. In the United States, $9,000 is $9,000. But in Canada, those extra interest charges aren't deductible. In the 25 percent federal tax bracket, you'll have to earn more than $14,000 in extra income to pay federal and provincial taxes and have enough net pay left over to cover the increase. Not to pay the mortgage. To pay the increase . . . from a 6 percent swing in interest rates!

Scary? Sure it is. But remember, at that point in the cycle, there are very few buyers around. You might not be able to sell the house. You certainly won't be able to sell it for the inflated values that made you feel so rich just a few percentage points ago. So you hang on until the market improves, which it does. But when the market improves, the house looks like a good investment again, and you hang onto it because there is nothing else you can do with your money that would earn such a handsome return. That's the way it goes. Around and around.

Now let's add one more catch to the euphoria of a hot housing market. While you're feeling so good about how much more your house is worth this year, look at your property tax bill and your insurance bill. Both of those costs tend to ride like leeches on soaring real estate values. The more valuable the property, the higher the tax bill. The more valuable the property, the more it costs to replace it and insure it.

In a strong urban housing market, the "profits" are illusory. They exist only if you leave the city. The costs, however, are real. As the paper value rises, the real costs of taxes and insurance rise with it. And the interest cycle keeps you trapped: on the hot side of the market, you don't feel like selling; on the downturn, it's very much harder to sell.

Housing inflation and interest rates work in tandem to make the homeowner rich on paper and poor in practice. It's a bit like those old Yap Islanders whose currency consisted of huge stone discs. Riches gave the lucky ones status, prestige, bad backs and hernias. And today, in suburbia, a boom in the housing market sets every homeowner off on a gleeful calculation of worth, then finally to wondering why, if he or she is so rich, does it sometimes feel like poor.

Every homeowner has done it at least once. Perhaps when the newspaper runs a feature on house values in the city. Perhaps when the neighbour sells his place or a realtor holds an open house down the block. It comes as a shock at first. That much? That's crazy. Then the calculator comes out. Let's see . . . if that place is worth . . . then ours ought to be . . . a little off that for lawyers and agents, and we still owe this much on the mortgage . . . that leaves . . . WOW! Impressive, isn't it?

Then you wonder why you need two incomes just to pay the mortgage. If you really made a $67,000 profit on the house last year, then why do you feel so poor?

ALTERNATIVES

While you're in a musing mood, with some idea of real estate prices and a calculator in hand, muse for a little while longer on the alternatives. Let's take, for example, the Toronto family who bought for $133,000 and could sell the next year for $200,000. We've already dismissed the alternative of selling out and finding another suitable house in Toronto; there's no financial gain in that and much to lose by way of the middlemen. Consider, instead, the alternative of leaving the city.

Just suppose they took that $100,000 (the original $33,000 down pay-

27

ment plus the one-year profit of $67,000 from inflation) and left.

In Vancouver, they could buy an average house for just under $132,000. With $100,000 in hand from the Toronto sale, they could buy the same house in Vancouver and require a $32,000 mortgage in place of the old $100,000 mortgage. The difference in indebtedness, $68,000, amounts to about $7,500 a year in interest payments (at 11 percent). Remember, though, that to pay out $7,500 in post-tax payments, they had to earn $12,000 in pre-tax income. Moving from Toronto to Vancouver might allow them to drop almost one full-time job from the family income.

In Halifax, they could buy an average house for $86,000. The proceeds from the Toronto sale would allow them to pay cash in Halifax and put $14,000 change in the bank. That means no mortgage payments ever again plus some investment income.

American homeowners, too, can profit by moving from high-cost cities to low-cost cities. The difference between a house in Boston and one in West Palm Beach is $71,500. The Bostonian could get richer and warmer with one move. Moving from Hartford, Connecticut, to Portland, Oregon, puts a profit of almost $93,000 in an average homeowner's pocket.

Now, extend the logic one more step, and see what can happen if our Toronto family moves to a small town, village or rural area. Here, housing prices run the gamut from cheap bungalows along the road to exclusive waterfront estates. Here, they might spend as much for a house as they spent in the city. Or they could spend a great deal less. Within 200 miles of Toronto, they could find an ordinary house on an acre of land for as little as $50,000. For $60,000, they could buy a house in town, on a serviced lot. They could live mortgage-free and invest the rest. The difference between their $200,000 Toronto house and a $60,000 house in small-town Ontario comes to about $14,000 a year. That's the take-home pay from an average job. That's enough to afford more theatre, more restaurants, more sports, more shopping – more of all the "urban" amenities than they could afford (or afford the time for) when they actually lived in the city.

That huge differential in housing costs is one of the motors driving what some see as the beginning of a new exodus from city to country places. John Herbers of *The New York Times* insists that the movement is not the same as the "back-to-the-land" movement of the early 1970s. It's not a small-town revival or a repopulation of the dwindling farm belt. It's not even a movement in the usual sense, because it has no centre, no leaders and no clear direction other than any direction at all that leads away from the cities. Herbers calls it a dispersal from high-density places to low-density places. Uncertain how to label the destinations of these new migrants, scattered as they are along country roads, lake and seashore, mountain and desert, Herbers coins the phrase "the new heartland."

We could draw key distinctions between the American movement and any similar stirrings in Canada. Certainly, some American cities have deteriorated further than Canadian ones. American cities are beset by more serious problems of poverty, class and racial tensions than are Canadian cities. Canadians have more wide-open spaces to move to and a wider range of public supports, like health insurance, to fall back on if a move proves inhospitable.

But, with a nod in the direction of those distinctions, it's easier to see the parallels. Houses really are sprouting in the most unlikely locations, both sides of the border. And the most unlikely people are moving into them. In part, it is the spreading of "commutersheds" around the big cities. But there isn't the same economic advantage in that. It's true that the newer, more distant suburbs may be cheaper than the inner suburbs or renovated downtown housing, but land prices rise in anticipation of the spreading suburb, not just with the beginning of construction. Outer suburbs really aren't that much cheaper. The economic impetus for industries and individuals is to move beyond the suburbs.

Where beyond the suburbs is a question that suddenly has a dozen factors of decision in place of the single one that set the old limits of the suburb. Once the daily commute from suburb to downtown business was broken, where to live became a function of where to find jobs, where to find the best weather and scenery, where the land is most affordable, where the gardening is ideal, where there is room for pets and where the locals are friendliest.

That's what makes it so hard for Herbers to put a pin in the map and say that's where people are moving. In fact, people, and the jobs that support them, are spreading out in patterns that have no single focus. They have many more dimensions than migrations we have seen before.

There are lots of other motors besides the economics of housing to drive the new migration. But economics is the big one. And oddly enough, for urbanites, it's the hardest one to see. The blind spot is the delusion that housing inflation can make the homeowner rich, that we can somehow stay in the city and profit from it too, eat the cake and have it. What's hard to see is that inflation drives up real costs and imagined profits. Those paper profits can't come to life unless you leave the city. But (and here's where the city dwellers are right) once you've left the merry-go-round, it's not so easy to get back on. If city prices continue to rise faster than the country property appreciates, then the gap (which was your profit on leaving) becomes the cost of reentry. And the gap could well be wider coming back in than it was on leaving. A move to the heartland might be a one-way trip.

If the thought of losing your toehold on the housing market is all that keeps you in the city, there are some strategies, which we will come to later, by which you can keep your money in the city while removing your body to more pastoral places. None of those strategies is entirely satisfactory, since few of us can afford to live that far from our money without worrying about how it's doing.

Better, by far, to have a close look at yourself first and try to figure out where you really want to live. Try this: Make a list of all the things you like best in life. Beside each activity, make a note of how often you actually enjoy it: golf – four times a year; the *Times* crossword – once a week; that kind of thing. Now, divide the list into those things which can only be done in the city versus the portable pleasures. You might, for example, list live opera as a city-only pleasure, which you now enjoy once a year; you play golf on a city course but know it can be played almost anywhere in North America; museum days are city items; dining out doesn't have to be in the city, but you may enjoy the variety there. Be honest about the frequency, though. If you're dining out in fast-food outlets, steak houses and ferny-plant places, they don't count. You can find them anywhere. Just count the number of times per year that you really do eat sushi or knish in the city.

If you've always lived in cities, the hard part will be deciding which of the pleasures do exist outside the walls. But go ahead, be tough. It may take you a few years to realize that there's world-class baroque music in Lamèque, one of the continent's best Inuit art galleries in Lunenburg, a great Basque restaurant in Elora, an excellent local beer in Vernon, a gigantic bookstore in Cobalt and good sports facilities almost anywhere.

But you don't know all that yet, so go ahead and list such things as purely city pleasures. The surprise, if you're honest, will be discovering the limited use you make of the facilities the city does offer. A woman from Montreal once told me that she didn't like Ottawa because there weren't enough restaurants. Then we counted and found that it would have taken her several lifetimes to try them all—new restaurants opened more often than she dined out. It's a bit like atomic bombs: after you have enough to wipe out the universe once, the rest are just for bragging. If a city has more pleasures than you can use, the surplus doesn't do a thing for your life.

Got the list? The list of strictly urban pleasures? Good. Now, consider the cost of living in the city compared with the cost of living someplace else, as we did a few pages ago with housing costs. What's the difference in your case? $10,000 a year? More? That's what it costs you to hang onto your urban investment. If the pleasures you get in return aren't worth that much, then maybe the investment isn't worth keeping. Your once-a-year trip to the opera may not be a $30 ticket after all; it may be a $10,000 ticket.

Now look at it the other way. If your fairy godmother were to offer you that $10,000 a year for life, what would you do with it? What would you buy? More leisure time? Early retirement? More living space? Those wishes may be more compatible with a strategic move to the country than with keeping your toehold in the urban market.

You might not be able to afford to go back to the same house you sold a few years before. But then, you probably can't afford to buy a house in Tokyo either. Or in Mexico City. Does that spoil your day?

COUNTRY PLACES

▼▼▼▼▼

This is not Utopia we're talking about. Utopia is a charming old house built to modern standards, on a sunny but shaded five-acre lot, surrounded by miles of protected parkland and yet only a short walk from world-class culture and entertainment. The house is right on the beach but high enough on the mountain for magnificent views. Closely sheltered from cold winter winds but open to summer breezes. Absolute privacy and lots of friendly neighbours nearby. That is Utopia. In the real world, of course, we may have to settle for some compromises.

Fortunately, one old and important compromise on the perfect choice has changed in recent years – the workplace. Rewarding employment is no longer the captive of the corporation and the city. There's a new growth in self-employment, small business, flexible hours, shared jobs, work-at-home arrangements and mid-career shifts to new skills and vocations. Perhaps even more significant is the corporate shift from mass production to smaller production units and the shift of these smaller units away from the cities and out to the small towns and countryside. With the new flexibility in employment possibilities, more people are free to look at the other elements of life.

For many of us, where to find work is no longer the simple question that precludes all the others. Now, at last, we can separate the questions and ask: Where do we want to sleep? Play? Learn? Talk with friends? If we want to sleep where there are fewer lights and noises, play where the beaches are cleanest, meet friends where entertainments are liveliest and – finally – work where it best suits our careers and interests, then meeting some of those separate goals in the choice of a place to live may now be possible.

What is certain, in the absence of Utopia, is that we will have to travel to one or more of those activities. We can try to minimize travelling time. But that doesn't mean what it used to mean. It used to mean living over the shop, in a factory row or in the suburb closest to work. Now it might mean nearest to recreation, nearest to schools, nearest to shopping or nearest to whatever is important. In the matrix pattern that life has taken, we can live just about anywhere within that web. The choice is now a matter of weighing all the factors: the cost of living, the quality of the view or the neighbours.

The first step, however, is to open the mind to all the possibilities and erase all the old stereotypes of what other places are like. They just aren't like that anymore.

The old stereotype divides the world simply into town and country, and it paints those two ideas into an even sharper dichotomy: big city with all its suburbs and then the family farm. If that neat division ever really lived, it has long since died.

URBAN IMAGES

Cities just aren't the same stew of mixed neighbourhoods, races, street life and marketplaces that they used to be. Mass culture and city planners have seen to that. There are more McBurger places in the city than the mix of charming little ethnic bistros that the stereotype recalls. And though the huge urban malls still have countless little shops, most sell Levi's and the fad cotton of the year. The diversity of the shops is an illusion. One shop might have a cuter name than the rest, a flashier window, but the goods on the shelves are much like the goods next door. That's not a general condemnation – there is still variety in the city. But it is not as diverse as it used to be, and it's not as diverse as we imagine it to be.

Some North American cities have indeed maintained or restored small core areas where the architecture is old and interesting and the shops small and diverse, where those charming bistros and street life really do abound. Those who spend their time there might base an image of the whole metropolis upon these districts, assuming that these few neighbourhoods are the city. They are the city for the few. Tourists, students and those who are able to afford the high rents in the core enjoy them, and suburbanites visit occasionally, if only when out-of-town guests want to see "the city."

Even in those metro areas with the best restored cores, however, the suburban majority live, shop and work where the street life is four lanes wide, the shops are in big malls and the local bistro has a big yellow M in front. That's the day-to-day reality of the large metropolis for most of those who live there.

Nor is the mix of people as rich as some would like to believe. Those industries that have not been priced out of city centres by the real estate boom have been zoned away by a generation of city planners whose tidy minds prefer to see the city all divided by function: shopping here, residential over there and factories out where noises and smells won't offend.

Take Lunenburg, Nova Scotia, for example. Arguably one of the prettiest towns on the Atlantic coast, pretty enough to be pictured on the hundred-dollar bill, Lunenburg pegs its charm on its old working heart. The core is a richly textured fabric of wharves, boatyards, chandlers, foundry, forge, residences and retail. No zoner would allow it to be built today. Most of what survives is a well-preserved anachronism. The new fish plant is miles out of town. An auto shop got the zoners' heave-ho five years ago. In 50 years, the charming working core of that town will be little more than a museum piece, a safe, odourless, inoffensive, profitable, high-priced tourist prop. The kind of people who once worked there won't be able to afford to live there.

Once the city is so neatly zoned, the dynamic is to intensify that functional apartheid with people divisions. The most shameful examples were the colour bars that divided cities by race. When blockbusting and twinges of social conscience drove the blatant colour bars underground, the homogeneous neighbourhoods preserved their purity with economic barriers that had the same effect. If the zoning bylaw insists that every house must have its individual 60-foot lot and only one family in residence, then that automatically excludes everyone below a certain income level. So modern cities have raised sharply distinct divisions between the poor, the working class, the middle class and the orthodontists.

Sometimes even money isn't enough to keep out anyone who might be a little bit different. Few urban neighbourhoods allow city folks to keep animals, unless, of course, the animals are of no use whatsoever. You can, for example, keep piranhas but not trout. Parrots but not chickens. A wolfhound but not a goat. A rabbit is all right as long as it has a name, but don't even think of lapin stew unless you want to risk the wrath of planners and neighbours.

Kanata, a fat nouveau suburb of Ottawa, zoned out television aerials and clotheslines! Honestly, you are not allowed to hang out the wash there. If you don't have a clothes dryer or cable, Kanata doesn't want you. Toronto neighbourhoods introduced substantial speed bumps so that the commuters couldn't drive through. The Glebe, in Ottawa, followed suit.

Much zoning works to segregate the modern city, undermining that very diversity which city lovers laud. That's one of the reasons cities no longer fit the old image of the rich and lively fabric of Dickensian London or Hemingway's Paris. Not even London and Paris are like that anymore.

The other big difference between the image and the reality of the city is the way in which we amuse ourselves. For most, the corner pub, coffeehouse, neighbourhood park and pool hall have ceded their former place to VCRs and home entertainment. Or mass entertainments. A night out is more likely to be a concert in the company of 20,000 others than a game of chess with the pensioners in the park. Even in the flesh, mass entertainment hardly represents the kind of intimate diversity that can make cities exciting. Popular entertainers can be as exciting on television as they are when seen from the 99th row of a football stadium.

And speaking of things like football, has it occurred to anyone else what absurd ironies have allowed urban mass entertainments to continue in spite of television? When big-screen, full-colour, slow-motion instant replays from a dozen camera angles kept sports fans at home where they could really see the game well, the stadiums emptied. You might pay $20 a ticket to sit in the front row, and I had a better view from my isolated farmhouse. I could see right into the huddle, sit on the bench, follow the play downfield, visit the locker room and see the best plays more than once. And there weren't any drunks pouring beer down my neck or jumping up to block my view with their "wave." So how did the owners respond? They put television screens into the stadiums. Now you can pay 20 bucks to sit at midfield and watch the game on the big television screen with 50,000 fellow fans. If that hasn't struck you as strange, then I have a bridge I'd like to sell you.

Mass entertainment, mass culture and mass merchandising have made cities and towns of all sizes more alike. Those differences which remain within the cities are too readily zoned into separate, homogeneous enclaves. And the automobile further isolates the urbanites from the city as it might have been and once was. It keeps them on the freeway in their boxes instead of mingling on the streetcars and sidewalks with their fellow cosmopolitans. And it takes them to Muzak malls rather than to the older, more diverse downtown where parking is an increasing problem.

Rural Images

If gas lamps and corner grocers no longer typify the city, what about popular rural images? Why is it wrong to think of the alternative to the city as a simple (some might say stultifying) bucolic life on the family farm?

To begin with, they aren't making family farms anymore. Like the corner grocer in the old city neighbourhood, the family farm has been taken over by a chain, expanded, geared to world markets and rebuilt with more capital than most families could legally accumulate in three generations. There are a few brave survivors. But the survivors have clung to the land by using one of the following strategies:

a) "Working out" or taking a regular job to support both family and the farm.

b) Expanding with borrowed capital and conscripted family labour to build the farm into a near-corporate operation.

c) Ignoring capital and labour costs, pretending that $2 an hour and 2 percent return on the value of the land and equipment is a business.

None of those strategies allows the simple, satisfying life style that is the stuff of storybook farms and cereal commercials. Is it any wonder that farmers suffer from more nervous ailments, ulcers and suicides than, say, bus conductors or postal sorters? If fickle markets and greedy bankers don't do you in, there are always the hazards of pesticide poisoning, barn lung and drought to worry about.

Farming is still a vital, worthy, honourable occupation. But it isn't a simple life, and it isn't easy to get into. In 1980, the average Canadian farm absorbed $339,000 in capital, and it returned $10,204 on that capital and a year's labour.

Fortunately, farming isn't the only alternative to high-rise living. Outside the city limits lies a panoply of living styles that ranges from wilderness homesteads to condo clusters in cottage country. Just about the only thing they have in common is low density – the fact of not being in the city. That is where the new diversity lies.

It wasn't always so, which in a way excuses those with fixed ideas of what rural life is like. But in the last decade or so, mass communication, mobile capital and fundamental shifts in the economy have changed the face of the country, creating the amazing mix of exurban development that John Herbers called "the new heartland." Unlike the old American heartland, which was rooted in the farm and in a homogeneous set of social, religious and political values, the new heartland is scattered and amorphous. It clusters in the mountains of Colorado, in Florida, Texas and the Carolinas. It goes wherever the scenery and the weather are better. And the jobs follow. While the cities in these areas have grown rapidly, Herbers points to an even more significant diffusion of people outside those cities: around the lakes, along the back roads and in much smaller communities. These aren't suburbs of the cities. In many cases, the growth is too far beyond the suburbs for daily commuting. It is certainly too far beyond the city limits for the kind of urban services that the old suburbs received. The new heartland, in Herbers' view, generates at least a part of its own employment. The new heartland, unlike the old, has money, mobility and education.

It is always risky to make close comparisons between the United States and Canada, but Herbers' views have echoes north of the border. He sees very little of the new growth in the American prairies, where agriculture still dominates. Similarly, exurban growth in Canada has bypassed the prairies in favour of the milder weather and diverse scenery of the Annapolis and Okanagan valleys, Vancouver Island, Quebec's Eastern Townships and parts of Ontario. Canada lacks a sun belt, but the exurban migration seems to follow many of the same driving forces that Herbers describes below the border.

The one thing that might be said for the exurban growth, north or south of the border, is that it is remarkably diverse in character, appearance, economies and values. There is no typical exurban community. Many don't have the legal and political boundaries that define older communities. Many aren't actually "communities," even in the loosest social sense.

Nevertheless, for the sake of urban readers who might still think of life outside the city as some narrow Mariposa, we should at least sample some of the variety to be found in the vital towns, villages and rural spaces.

SMALL CITIES

Demographers might draw the line between towns and cities at a population level of about 10,000. The numbers really don't mean very much, however. The numbers depend on where you draw the city limits, and politicians like to draw them way out there in order to look as big as possible. Like Brisbane, Australia. When Brisbane's population was about 650,000, boosters told anybody who would listen that the city was the second largest in the world. Of course, the city limits were set so far back of beyond that there was more kangaroo poop than people in the outer suburbs. And apartments in the centre of the city still had a few outdoor privies. But it was larger in land area than Paris or New York. The idea that bigger is better is partly a throwback to tail-fin mentality and partly a ploy to qualify for larger grants. But who cares? What we are considering is the notion that some places are better and cheaper places to live than some other places, and the demographers' numbers may mean less than the character of a place.

The problem is that people who live in cities with big populations find it hard to believe that cities with smaller populations can enjoy all the same amenities that the big guys have. Often, the amenities are simply closer together and less costly in small cities. As we've seen in "Paper Riches, Pauper Lives," a move from Toronto to Vancouver could put $68,000 into the pocket of the average Toronto homeowner. Now, let's be honest. It is true that you cannot see Rochester, New York, from Vancouver . . . not on the clearest day. But the view from Vancouver's Grouse Mountain is at least as good as the view from the CN Tower. And there is enough nightlife and culture to keep that $68,000 at least as busy as it was in Toronto. And transplants can still watch *The National* at night and feel as if they're right back in Toronto, at the centre of things.

Vancouver, however, still feels like a big city to some of us. Look at some place even smaller. Look at a place like Kingston, Ontario, population 60,000. It's an easy walk from Queen's University, at the top of the hill, through the centre of the city to the yacht harbour on the other side. In summer, you can sit on the terrace of an old hotel and watch the sails come in from the lake or take a short walk up Princess Street for a choice of summer theatre. Guddle through the aisles of a rare-book store, stop to listen to the repertoire of the adolescent sidewalk saxophonist, or choose from scores of restaurants. You can read an excellent local daily, which carries the same wire-service stories that *The Globe and Mail* or *The New York Times* carries. You can watch Canadian or American national networks, listen to live jazz or stroll back up the hill to check the overflowing bulletin boards for public lectures, excursions or sports.

Those who love cities usually draw the ideal as some meeting of diversity or a place where cultures, interests and ideas meet face to face in streets and public forums. The truth is that smaller cities, like Kingston, come closer to that ideal than larger cities. Walk up to a stranger on Yonge Street or Times Square, and ask the meaning of life. You might lose your wallet, your innocence, or both. You're more likely to scare the bejesus out of the stranger. But the odds on engaging that stranger in some meaningful encounter might be better back in Kingston. A city of its size is still forum size, still small enough to walk around. It has a people life on streets that have not been abandoned to expressways, derelicts and commercial sex.

Having a hundred times as many people would not help Kingston one whit. It would just make it harder to move around. Athens, at the time of Socrates, wasn't much bigger.

There are many others: St John's, Halifax, Saskatoon, and on and on. The liveliest of them share a few common features: they are far enough from bigger cities to remain independent, they have a diverse economic base, a university, a geographic focus and a cultural focus.

The distance from larger cities is the difference between an interesting small city and an incorporated suburb of the metropolis. That distance allows the diversity that creates the interest. No matter how blessed it is, a small city that lives too close to a larger one becomes submerged, becomes a dormitory, becomes a Markham to Toronto. Its residents, whether or not they work in the larger centre, come to depend on it for entertainment, culture, recreation and information. Those amenities then wither in the smaller place.

A diverse economic base does two things. First, it provides some long-term economic stability to the city. A city built around a mine or a single industry (like automobiles) lasts only as long as the ore or only as long as the technology in the factories. One-industry cities with short lives do not build facilities for the future. Secondly, a broad economic base attracts a wider variety of skills and people to the city. When a single industry dominates, that subject dominates everything else, right down to the conversation at parties. That's one of the things that makes government towns dull. There may be lots of important or exciting activity, but when everyone works at the same place, the homogeneity is deadly. It's the difference between a forest and a tree plantation.

A university, like a diverse economy, brings a continual supply of new blood and new ideas to the city. On a more practical level, a university supplies a great deal of unattached energy. Many of these people don't have to stay home with the kids at night or clean out the gutters. The free energy and diversity of interest spawn a wide and accessible array of activities: chamber concerts, film societies, hang-gliding clubs, debates, parties, fringe politics and just plain nonsense . . . anything to mop up all that youthful libido. The host city both suffers and enjoys the excess.

Geographic focus seems at first to be an odd item on the list of things that make small cities interesting. Cities are supposed to be about people. Only secondarily have they come to be defined as buildings and streets. Geography, however, does what streets and buildings cannot do. It gives the city its natural centre, the sun about which the rest revolves. Halifax and St. John's have their harbours. Ottawa has the Hill, Quebec its cliff and old town. But where is Winnipeg's natural centre? Portage and Main? A street corner? Where is Calgary's? Under the Husky Oil Tower? Regina has its artificial lake, but Saskatoon, cut by a natural river valley, has more focus. I confess that I don't know why topography makes interesting cities. And my evidence for saying that it does is personal and therefore limited. It just seems to be so.

Cultural focus is even harder to define, in part because it can be so many things: an annual festival, a home for performing arts or a particularly lively press. It might be drama in St. John's, Shakespeare in Stratford, ballet in Winnipeg, Acadiana in Moncton or rodeo in Calgary. Rare is the small city that could support a complete and cosmopolitan culture, but blessed is the small city that nevertheless has something uniquely its own. That cultural specialty, if we can call it that, is the thing that makes small cities different from one another, diverse in a way that one-of-everything McTropolises cannot be.

There are limits to the small city too. Almost by definition, we can say that small cities won't be sufficient for cosmopolitan appetites. You might have to go elsewhere for big league baseball, the best seafood or grand opera. Indeed, any small city that tried to be New York on a minor scale would be as misguided as those Chinese/Canadian/ steakseafoodandpizza-specialty restaurants, where the menu runs to 20 pages and everything tastes the same. A small city must be more the boutique than the department store. That's what makes it special. But it also means that small-city residents have to travel if they want to sample others' specialties.

But then, if you think about it, that's true of big cities too. Foreign theatre is difficult to find in New York and won't be found at all on the famous Broadway, which serves up little but its own bland pablum of American musicals. Nor do New Yorkers have easy access to South American literature, Quebec's cuisine, good television news or rodeo. Any New Yorker who remains in the self-proclaimed centre of the universe and thinks he has seen it all is as narrow and provincial as those Hollywood cultural cripples who believe that the Oscars go to the best in cinema.

I digress. We were talking about the limits of the *small* city and the fact that those who live there know their hometowns are not the centre of the universe. Forced to recognize a wider world, outside their own, they may be more truly cosmopolitan than the self-satisfied, unmoving urbanite.

I still digress. There really are some limits to small cities. Chief among them are those same limits that handicap the larger cities. Residential land is scarce, carefully controlled in its use and expensive to occupy. If you want more room, more control or more of it all for the same price, then look at even smaller towns and villages.

SMALL TOWNS

There are nearly 10,000 small towns and villages in Canada. A few are dying, a few are booming, and most of them have stayed about the same. But while the size may have remained the same, the character and economy of these small places are not at all what they used to be.

The mechanics of modern, small-town life are not very different from those of metropolitan life. Small towns with fewer than 10,000 people still have public water and sewer services, cable television, franchise fast food, malls and chain stores. Towns of 5,000 have apartment buildings and local cleaning services. Aside from the taxi, there is little in the way of public transportation, but in any town of fewer than 10,000 people, just about any place is within walking distance.

Look at a town like Perth, Ontario, population just under 6,000. Barely a kilometre by two, the town is compact enough that residents can walk to work, recreation and shopping in less time than it takes to park in many cities. Within a few blocks, Perthites enjoy an 18-hole golf course, tennis courts, five banks, liquor and beer stores, a large supermarket, health food, variety stores, clothing stores, hardware stores, two bakeries, three travel agents, two bookstores, video outlets, half a dozen decent restaurants and a couple of superior ones, a public library, a post office, churches, a museum, a funeral home, a horse track and stables, an electronics store, an art gallery, appliance centres, two sports stores, three drugstores, dentists, doctors, a hospital, sundry drinking establishments, a community centre and rink, indoor and outdoor swimming pools, playgrounds, parks, a building-supply store, a community college, four schools, ball diamonds, a toboggan hill, boat docks, a theatre (live), a fitness centre, a dance studio – we could go on, but why gild lilies?

Look at the list, abbreviated as it is, and test those amenities against your own needs. What's missing? What would you need, on a regular basis, that isn't within an easy stroll from anywhere in Perth? An Algerian restaurant? An international airport? An Olympic diving tower? Those less frequently needed facilities are an hour's drive away. In London, England, it would take more time to travel by bus or taxi from Oxford Street shops to a "central" residential district like Islington. But a common row house in Islington would set you back $600,000 or more because it's so central. Think about it.

Now, test that catalogue of Perth-sized services against the old image of small-town Canada. Farm-based economy? There are more travel agencies than feed stores in Perth. Meatloaf and raisin-pudding cuisine? It's easier to find falafel here. Unlettered yokels? Some, but not enough to hurt attendance at the library, theatre, museum and bookstores. I've found *The Economist* on local shelves, Cicero (in Latin) at a local bookstore and, indeed, a few characters who mangle the language with bumper-sticker discourse. Oddly enough, the latter, when seen as people and not as types, make as rich and interesting a contribution to the social fabric as any of the rest.

Employment is diversified across more than a dozen small manufacturing plants and the usual mix of service industries. The employers include local entrepreneurs and small branches of large multinationals like 3M, Jergens, Wampole and Westinghouse, attracted here by the same low prices and pleasant surroundings that make it a nice place for people. The industrial diversity is wide enough that the closure of any one plant wouldn't be enough to threaten the town.

And the industrial base is sophisticated enough to bring professional-level careerists from outside the town. Sophisticated enough, in turn, to allow local youngsters access to career paths that start in the hometown and can lead through hierarchies to any place they want to go. The prospects for a livelihood and a lively mix of neighbours are as great here as they are in the city. Not every small town is so lucky, but anyone who contemplates a move to smaller places should know that they are not all stagnant backwaters.

But if the old stereotypes no longer apply, what is life really like in a place like that? Everyday life? What makes it different from the city? Are the differences only in the numbers? Or is there some distinctive quality of life?

There are as many little distinctions between them as there are little towns. But at the root of all those little things is the one big difference that is the blessing and the bane of nearly every little town. Here it is: Small-town life is more public than city life. I've chosen the word carefully because it means more than one thing.

It means, first, that there is less privacy in a little place, less anonymity. If you cherish secret vices, or even secret virtues, forget it. You can practise vice or virtue as you wish, but not in secret and not for long.

Some years ago, I opened a small-town bank account. There wasn't much to it: a few dollars, a signature and a safety deposit box. I barely knew the town, had never been in the bank and didn't know a soul on the other side of the counter. Aside from the signature, it was the simplest, most anonymous transaction imaginable. A week later, I went back to leave some papers in the safety deposit. As I put my hand in my pocket to fish out the box number and key, the clerk, whom I hadn't even seen on the previous visit, went straight to the proper box without checking the file.

In the years since, I have felt both warm and worried about episodes like that. Warm last year, when we went away on vacation and accidentally overdrew the account. No costly or embarrassing NSFs resulted. The bank staff remembered we were away, adjusted the accounts and mailed a polite reminder. That's the good news. The bad news is that I haven't a hope of ever supporting a mistress or sending money to the IRA in secret.

Secondly, the public character of the small town imparts a different sense of responsibility over time. Behaviour has to be more considerate. It is one thing to lose your temper with the clumsy waiter who spills soup in your lap in the city. A quick retort, a curse on all his children, get it out of your system, and it's done. It is quite another thing to behave like that in a small town. There, you'll likely see the waiter on the street once a week for the next 20 years or see him grow up and marry your daughter, or you'll sit next to his brother at the Rotary luncheon: "You know, old Harold still talks about the day that he spilled the soup in your lap and you cussed him out like a drunken sailor."

Small-town memories last forever, and any unusual behaviour enters the infinite folklore. That's one of the reasons small-town folks are known to be so much more polite than city people. Here, a harsh remark is not for the moment but a thing that lasts forever. In that way, small-town life is more like a marriage, in which slights might be forgiven but rarely forgotten and you learn not to hurt someone so close.

Finally, small-town life is more public in the sense that it is more integrated, less divided into compartments. In the city, you might work in one district, live in another and play in a third. You might have one set of friends from work, another in the neighbourhood and a separate group you see at sport. Those paths don't cross. That's impossible in a smaller place. All paths cross. Work and play and neighbourhood aren't so easily separated into distant institutions. The result is that life is less bureaucratized. Those who administer don't have the anonymity it takes to act in impersonal, bureaucratic ways.

From that basic difference – the integration of life's institutional parts into a more personal, public whole – spring other differences.

Funerals are more important in small towns, because you will know more older people; they aren't segregated away.

The newspaper – the local weekly – is a central organ of small-town life. It's important not so much for the news as for the names: who's birthed, who's engaged, who's wrecked the car and who's having an anniversary. Little things. As with family letters, the readers may already know the story, but seeing it written still matters.

Small-town life is much like a large, extended family. For newcomers, it's more like marrying into a large, extended family. You're the new in-law, confused, appalled and intrigued by the web of family connections and the vast social history of good deeds, slights, crazy aunts, who said what, family secrets, attic treasures, code words and a closeness that can be cloying if it embraces you, cliquish if it does not. If you like that kind of family life, you'll love small towns. If, on the other hand, you hated family reunions and like being alone, think twice before plunging in cold.

Village life

Any distinction between small town and village must, of necessity, be fuzzy. Having 100 or 1,000 or 5,000 people doesn't change the essential family character of a place. Every town and country crossroad has a personal touch that can be prying or caring, depending, in part, on how you react to it. But some things are different in the smaller communities – practical differences that mean more than the numbers. Rather than base the distinctions on population (4,999 people act like this, 5,001 act like that), let's consider life in smaller places in terms of the amenities offered and the proximity to other places.

For the sake of convenience, let's call places with piped water and sewers "towns." Communities that rely on individual wells and septic tanks, we'll call "villages." Not a flawless distinction but useful.

A well and septic tank in the open countryside are not without risk – agricultural chemicals, surface runoff, underground sulphur and other minerals that can leave a bad taste (and more) in the mouth. But in a village, where lots of wells and flushers share backyard space, the possibilities for bad water, bad smells and bad feelings multiply like window flies on a warm, spring day.

If you've ever lived in a city house, you'll be familiar with the snowstorm wars. That's when you shovel the walk and pile the snow on the narrow strip between you and the next-door neighbour. Then he shovels his path, and the pile between you gets higher. Eventually, it spills over. His tossings land on your walk, and vice versa. You can escalate the war with snow blowers, but the effect is the same. You cannot pile it high enough and straight enough to suit two close neighbours after one big storm. Now, imagine that the pristine snow is, instead, sewage. The fact that the piles may be mostly underground merely reduces the boiling feelings to a longer simmering feud. Sooner or later, it bubbles over.

That doesn't happen in every village, but it happens often enough that you should ask before you buy. Ask the local health inspector, not the real estate agent.

Smaller places lack other amenities that may not seem so important until you have to drive 50 miles to get them: a supermarket (the local grocery may be priced for the summer cottage trade, not year-round, weekly provisioning); a school (sure, the bus comes, but what about after-school sports, clubs and meetings?); a bank (you can't do it by phone); a hardware store (it's one thing to drive to a distant town to shop for clothes, quite another when you're one bolt short in the middle of a vital repair).

Village houses are generally cheaper than town houses. The taxes may be lower, the gardens bigger, the scenery and wild places closer at hand. But a village is not such a convenient place for conducting the everyday business of life.

Most of all, village life is closer than town life and closer than life farther out in the country. If town life is akin to the extended family of in-laws, village life is more like moving in with the in-laws. How close? Richard and Rosemary moved from New York City to Lombardy, Ontario, a village barely big enough to support one general store and a phone booth. Friends from New York, driving through the area, saw the sign for Lombardy and decided to pay a call. They found Richard's number in the local phone book and called from the pay booth by the general store.

"Surprise!"

They explained the finding of the village and where they were calling from.

"Now how do we find your house?"

"Hang up," Richard directed, "then dial this same number again. Step out of the phone booth and listen. The house with the ringing phone is ours."

That's how close village life can be. You can't walk around in your underwear. And you can't make many mistakes about choosing a compatible set of neighbours.

In a larger place, the range of people is wide enough that you can expect to pick your friends and speak politely to all the rest when you meet them on the street. In a town of 5,000, you'd have to be very particular if you couldn't find enough like-minded souls for a full social life. In a village of 500, the choices are fewer and the contacts more frequent. You see the same few people more often. If you don't get along with them, village life will be a misery. If you like to sleep in and the neighbours target shoot on Sunday mornings, it's not going to work. If you like flower gardening and the summer evening corkball/kick-the-can/capture-the-flag encroaches on your pansies, then it's not going to work. Not well.

Village life can be very rich – for those who relish that much intimacy – but it takes as much tolerance as living with the in-laws. Pick your village slowly and with care.

There is one other difference between town and village that bears consideration. The town, with a more or less full set of shops and services, tends to be the focus of everyday life for those who live and work there. Townsfolk still go to the city for fancy shopping or a big night out, but the banking, the groceries, school activities and casual recreation all centre in one place. The village, on the other hand, has more limited amenities. So villagers, like real country dwellers, have to drive to nearby towns for shopping, recreation and other necessities. The villager, according to academic studies, is more likely to use a wide set of centres, shopping in this town, working in that one and travelling someplace else for entertainment.

The logic of these patterns may not be immediately obvious. It isn't always a matter of distance. Placing yourself in a village equidistant from three small towns does not mean that the services of those towns will be equally accessible. Political boundaries, utility-fee structures, school-district maps and long evolution impose certain patterns on the rural matrix.

Evolution? What sort of social Darwinism operates outside the city? Start with the premise that no small town can afford to be complete, at least not in the urban sense. Superior schools, recreation, shopping, entertainment, employment possibilities – at any one time, any small town might excel at any one of those things but not at all of them. A town of 3,000 might have one or two good restaurants and a smattering of cafés, but there won't be enough trade to support much more than that, unless the good restaurants attract diners from out of town. The out-of-towners need not be full-fledged tourists but can be visitors from the villages and rural places within driving distance. The better the restaurants, the more visitors come to dine in the town. The town that excels in restaurants can, thanks to the neighbours, support more and better restaurants than the town by itself could justify. So small towns tend to specialize in services that are good enough to attract outsiders. A small town blessed with a fine beach or scenic attraction will become the area's weekend leisure centre. A town with old money may have the most banks and investment brokers. A town with more young people might offer better cinema than other towns in the district. Whatever it is that sparks the initial move toward one specialty or another, the result is that little towns develop differences. And the people who live around little towns exploit those differences. And as they exploit the differences, the special advantage of each town becomes even more distinct. Usage breeds distinction, and the distinction shapes the usage.

Before you decide on this village rather than that one, ask the people who live there where they shop, where they work, join clubs, curl, eat out and go to the movies. Then ask why. The universe of surrounding towns is as important to the village as the village itself.

All in all, villagers use a wider matrix of other places than townies do – more driving in their lives to find more diversity. On the other hand, the village itself is a closer, more confined society. Sounds like a contradiction, but it's not. People who live in very small houses tend to spend more time in the garden, no matter how nice that little house

49

might be. People who live in very small houses with their in-laws tend to spend nearly all their time in the garden or beyond. Think about it.

RURAL PLACES

Smaller even than the villages but not at all confined, these are the single houses that follow back roads, cling to mountainsides and nestle down in woods – as independent as old-fashioned farms but without the fields and barns. The homestead. The one-house town. Sneerers call it strip development when it gets too close together, a village when it sprouts a little commerce, a town when it begins to collect taxes.

But that comes later, if at all. What we're talking about here is the first unruly collection of people outside the kraal. Not farms. Real farms are more places of business than places to live today. Call them hobby farms, small holdings, rural lots or whatever. They are best described in the negative: not watered, sewered or serviced; not joined in any official community; not joined in any physical way except by road, shore or the common view. These are the country places of today.

It's hard to measure the growth of such a movement and call it a trend. When enough people move to a country district, demographers relabel it "suburb" or "town," and those people vanish from the rural column. Despite the demographers' little diddle, the numbers say that our eyes haven't deceived us; something significant is happening out there. In Canada, the rural, nonfarm population formed 15 percent of the total in 1931, 17 percent in 1956 and 20 percent in 1981.

In the United States, the nonmetropolitan population grew by 16 percent during the 1970s. During the same decade, big cities and suburbs grew by only 10 percent.

The new rural dwellers work in nearby towns. They commute from country houses to the same kinds of jobs that any random collection of suburbanites would hold. They don't commute much farther. They certainly spend no more time commuting.

There are, however, some significant differences between country living and suburban or even village life. Here are a few:

In general, the cost of rural housing is lower than anyplace else. Land prices rise where there's water frontage or magnificent views. Otherwise, the farther you are from other people, the less you will pay for the land. It will cost more to drill the well and install the septic system, more to insure the house because you're farther from the fire department and possibly a little more interest on the mortgage because rural property is less convenient for those who foreclose and resell. And, if you're really building far from neighbours, you might have to pay a premium to extend the telephone and power lines. But the basic cost of the land is almost always less when you avoid the crowd.

The extent of the savings on rural housing is too individual a matter to average, but consider this: the extra costs (well, insurance and so on) apply to the house, not to the land. One house on a hundred acres engenders the same costs as a house on a single acre or an unserviced village house on a 40-foot lot. The difference is in the cost of the land. And the cost, per acre, is cheaper in the country.

Even property taxes are based not on the amount of land you hold but on its assessed value. Thus rural taxes are less per acre than village taxes.

The net result is that even village people can save by moving farther out. They can trade their village investment for more land, for a better house, or both.

The economics of a particular move are relatively easy to measure. But the important differences between town and country have little to do with numbers. These are the personal, subjective, emotional preferences that lie behind the decision to pull up stakes and find a quieter place. Calvin Beale of the U.S. Department of Agriculture has studied the recent urban-to-rural trend. "Every survey of newcomers to nonmetropolitan areas," he says, "has shown that the great majority give social reasons for their move rather than economic reasons."

In Canada, academic Janet Momsen asked a group of rural Albertans about their reasons for moving to a rural area. The economics of cheaper land made the list but were way behind the more important social reasons. The most common reason cited was that people just plain preferred to live in the country. Others wanted privacy, a better environment for their children or room to keep animals.

For those who want to move out of the crowd, the first question is, How far out? The answer is not necessarily "as far as possible." Remember, first, that there is no smooth continuum between the village and the country house. A country house is not a village of one. It's a different animal altogether. Take the lack of privacy that, for many, is the hardest fact of village life. If we could somehow plot pri-

51

vacy on a population graph, we would see lots of privacy in the anonymity of a big city. Then the privacy level would drop as we moved along the axis to smaller cities, drop farther still in the small towns and fall almost to zero in the village. Take one more step beyond the village, however, and privacy doesn't disappear. It shoots back up to city levels and beyond. A country house can be as antisocial as you want it to be. You can have as many secrets as you can in a city apartment – without the need to whisper.

There is more latitude for just about anything outside the village: less concern about building restrictions, animal restrictions and noise restrictions. Even those things which are legal in the village, like mowing the lawn early Sunday morning, might be frowned upon to such an extent that villagers restrict themselves out of plain old neighbourly consideration. Or they violate the unwritten laws only to risk the harsher penalties of social censure. Beyond the village, there are fewer such considerations.

Beyond the village, you can garden in the nude, howl at the moon and keep pet skunks if you like. The gossips will be delighted, but the only ones offended will be your own family and perhaps the postman. Teacher Marty Rennick moved away from neighbours so that he could install a runway for his plane beside the house. Auctioneer Don Raffan started family life in a cramped trailer, steps away from the office. When he finally moved to the foot of a mountain wild enough for eagles and bears, he bought enough land to put a full-sized rodeo ring in the backyard. Now when he gets home at the end of the day, he saddles up and ropes calves for a while to relax.

Some like to see wildlife wandering through the yard. Others enjoy the night sky never seen by those who live with streetlights. Some like to ski from the back door into the woods, and others want room to keep a horse. Most simply enjoy the peace and quiet and freedom from intrusion that country living allows. For us, the pleasure is having the space to grow 53 kinds of flowers and more food than we can eat, meadows and trees as far as we can see, no other lights but ours at night and no noise more abrasive than an overhead loon and the occasional passing snowmobile. In the first year here, I heard a train whistle blow in the middle of the night and felt violated, until someone pointed out that the train blew its whistle for the crossing in the town, nine miles distant. Poor town.

There are costs, of course. There are the direct financial costs already mentioned. And there are the social costs of seeing the neighbours less often. At my age, that's a price I readily pay. My teenagers disagree. So we drive them around to fill the social gap, and that adds to the financial costs. In a couple of years, we'll all be happy.

REAL ESTATE DRUNKS

It is only human to overreact when given a chance at wish fulfill-ment. That's why kids get sick on the bottomless chocolate Easter basket, why adults turn a perfectly civilized martini into a two-day drunk and why people who yearn for a place in the country go shop-ping for something the size of Alaska. That is especially true of peo-ple accustomed to living in cities. It's the astonishing difference in the price of land that turns urbanites into real estate drunks.

Sober second thought says that too much land is a burden – a lit-tle burden on the tax bill and a much bigger burden when it comes down to taking care of the place. Even seemingly wild forest has to be fenced, thinned and tended if it's to be productive. Insects, para-sitic vines, beaver dams and hungry porcupines can reduce the value of a hardwood forest in a few untended years. A forest has to be fenced against livestock that would eat young trees and trample them down to meadow. And meadows have to be mown if you want to keep them from reverting to forest. No matter how perfect the piece of land is, it won't stay the way it is unless you work at it. Nature constantly changes every untended landscape, even lakes and rivers. So decide how much you can tend, and avoid buying more.

It is equally important to restrain yourself from buying the wrong kind of land. Take farms, for instance, the first thought of many fed-up urbanites. Farms, especially farms with animals on them, demand constant attention. The more kinds of animals, the wider variety of crops, the more work involved for the farmer. It might be reward-ing work, in a spiritual sense if not in a financial one. But don't kid yourself that farm families have much time to romp in the meadows and smell the roses.

All right, you say, I'll buy just a small farm and keep it simple: a few head of cattle, maybe a pony for the kids, a big vegetable gar-den and a small plot of oats or something so that it still seems like a farm (and so that it can be taxed at reduced farm rates). The biggest difference between an operation like that and a real farm is the assured disappearance of any possibility of profit. You'll have almost the same amount of work, almost the same amount of capital but almost nothing by way of a crop to sell in the fall.

It's the same amount of work, because it retains the essential elements of a real farm. The fences still need to be fixed and the ditches cleaned, the barn still needs to be roofed, the laneway ploughed, the woodlot thinned, the pasture seeded, fed and weeded, the hay cut, raked and baled, the field (even a little field) turned, harrowed, seeded, weeded, combined, ploughed again and fed. Unless you have an awful lot of time to devote to this enterprise, all those small-farm chores require a tractor and a piece of equipment for nearly every task. You can rent equipment or call in custom crews, but that's another burden on the operating costs. It is costs that kill the mini-farm. The machinery costs the same whether you plough 10 acres or 100. But returns are in proportion to size—the 10-acre field produces one-tenth as much as the 100-acre field.

Farm animals are even harder to scale down than crops. Even with *one* cow, you have to be there every day. You can't take Bossy to the kennel when you want a weekend away.

Aha, you say, there are some small crops more suited to labour-intensive agriculture: berries, vegetables, orchards, asparagus or herbs. Smaller acreage, smaller machinery and smaller investment. All true. And the returns, per acre, can be higher. True. But the "labour-intensive" side of the equation is not an economist's abstraction. It's an aching back as you realize that an acre of tomatoes is an enormous amount to pick between now and tomorrow when they'll be too rotten to sell. It's a shock when you learn that weeds grow too close to vegetables to be pulled by machines and that only the hands will do (so *that's* why they don't grow this crop on big farms!). It's a quiet struggle with the values that brought you out of the city when you're told the only way to sell the apples is to spray them with poisons you were determined to avoid.

Jan and Dennis got tired of their jobs as teachers and "retired" to a little fruit and vegetable farm near Yarmouth, Nova Scotia. Dennis was no naïve boy from the city, though he had lived in some. It's just that the speed at which a strawberry ripens had never been part of his life before. If he had ever thought of the overnight change from green to red to soft little spots of rot, the thought was a positive one . . . yum yum. They picked the first crop by the lights of the pickup truck parked at the edge of the field. They picked until they ached and then picked some more.

Lots of people, like Jan and Dennis, make a living from small crops and mini-farms. It can be a satisfying and sometimes a profitable way to live in the country. But don't ever ever *ever* buy a farm with the thought that it can be a profitable hobby. It can be profitable or a hobby, but rarely both.

Now the good news and the bad news begin to converge. The bad news is that some farms can't support the farmers who work them. The good news is that those same farms can be wonderful places to live – if you have other means of support. The trick is to avoid trying to farm them so seriously that you go broke. You can grow all the vegetables and berries you want for family, friends and neighbours. But anything much more serious than that can become a major commitment of money, or labour, or both.

Farms that no longer make sense in the agricultural market can make supremely good sense in the real estate market. Consider, for a moment, the several factors that make a poor farm a loser in the food economy:

Size. Modern machinery and methods are too sophisticated and too expensive to warrant occasional use on small plots. Profitable farms are usually big farms. The 100-acre family farm may still be possible where the soil is rich, the farmer skilled and all other factors of production positive. But where those conditions have prevailed in the past, the successful small farmer has expanded, absorbing neighbouring farms and growing to a size that can justify the modern machinery. In many cases, the expansion of the best farm in the district absorbed the neighbour's fields but left the house and a few surrounding acres untouched. What remains is too small to farm but might still have an orchard, garden, woodlot, stream or view – all the amenities that made it a good building site in the first place.

Even if the marginal farm is still 50 or 100 acres, chances are that those acres no longer enjoy any financial independence. They've been leased to the most successful neighbour or abandoned to the forest. In either case, it might still be a good place to live. You can continue leasing fields to the neighbour or simply enjoy the forest.

Soil. The quality of the soil itself can change for a number of reasons: erosion removes the topsoil, overuse exhausts its fertility, airborne pollutants or extensive irrigation can change the chemical balance. Each diminution of quality reduces profits, until the land is taken out of production.

Changing technology can alter the criteria by which soil is judged good or bad. Helen Parsons, in her study of marginal agriculture, points out that "early settlers in some areas of Renfrew County consciously chose upland shield areas, rejecting the heavy but level and rock-free lowland areas. The upland soils, though shallow and rocky, were lighter and more easily worked using 19th-century methods." Those methods (notably the one-horse plough) are no longer competitive, and so many of those upland shield farms have been judged unprofitable and taken out of production, though they may still be very fine places to live and garden and build a measure of self-sufficiency.

Topography. The lie of the land makes its own contribution to the line between a farm where one can make a good living and those other farms that are merely good for living. High ground, steep ground, rocky ground, land cut by lakes and streams, all make life difficult for the modern commercial farmer and make the scenery extra interesting for the rest.

Marginal farmland is often cheaper than good farmland, often available in smaller parcels than the good farmland and often more scenic than the good farmland. That's as it should be. No use wasting a good view on the blind eyes of potatoes. And no use wasting good cropland on lawns and septic beds. In the truly rural areas, the market makes a just distribution.

The loss of farmland is rightly regretted in those cases where good, productive fields have been paved for suburbs and parking lots. But that's not the case here. That's more likely to be a city phenomenon, where agricultural profits can't compete with soaring land prices. In truly rural areas, land prices and suburban pressures don't force farmers out of business; the high cost of machinery and the low price of food force farmers out of business. The land is pushed out of production because the unit is too small or because the land isn't suitable for farming.

Like many others, we moved to the country imagining a farmlike life. Our initial criteria included pastures and some tillable acreage. We had some vague idea of using a cheap, secondhand tractor to produce at least one cash crop. Not full-time farming, but just enough to make use of the land and a little easy money.

The land we could afford was, of course, marginal: shallow and rocky, with shoulders of sandstone heaving through the crust. The land had been abandoned for more than a dozen years when we first saw it. The fields told their own story. Every acre or two centred on an outcropping of bedrock, mounded higher still with gathered

56

fieldstone. At the margins, fences teetered along more ridges of stone, painstakingly piled by a century of frustrated ploughmen. Among the stones was a litter of broken parts, adding their own testimony of frustration.

It never should have been a farm. Nature prefers to grow trees on land like this. A hundred years and many generations fought against that truth and lost. They gave up before we got here. That's what made the land affordable. Still, we had this idea that farms should have fields. We tried goats. They preferred the young trees to the old fields, and they would never be the easy crop we had in mind. Life has been easier since we accepted the inevitable, planted trees and let nature do it her way. There's still one field we're stubbornly hanging onto. It has only one rock pile and one swamp in its two acres. "The good field," we call it. It is still much more than we need.

HOW MUCH LAND DO YOU NEED?

Really need? How much you might need for privacy and to ensure that a McBurger isn't built next door is between you and your banker. I'm talking about those other things that people have in mind when they move to the country: growing vegetables and firewood, planting windbreaks or maybe fattening a little meat for the table. We associate those things with "farm" life, but do we need a real farm to do all that? Fortunately, no.

No numbers can be absolute, since so much depends on how fertile the soil is, how harsh the climate and how clever the hand of the grower, but let me throw out just enough numbers to give you a rough idea.

First, vegetables. Anybody who has ever grown a vine-ripe tomato beside the back door knows the yearning to do more. The question is, How much more? How much can one family easily care for? How much can one family eat? And how much land do you need for that?

Helen and Scott Nearing fed six vegetarians in Vermont on a third of an acre of garden space. Richard Langer reckoned that a 100-by-100-foot plot would feed a family of four plus guests. John Tobe, gardening in British Columbia, managed a year-round vegetable supply from a garden 65 by 110 feet, about a sixth of an acre. Here in eastern Ontario, our 90-by-75-foot patch feeds the four of us plus a steady stream of visiting teenage appetites. That provides a 12-month supply of potatoes, corn, tomatoes, green beans,

57

navy beans, broad beans and kidney beans, yellow and green onions, cantaloupe, carrots, cabbage, broccoli, Brussels sprouts, garlic, cauliflower, rhubarb, strawberries, asparagus, beets, squash, turnips, radishes, lettuce, chard, kohlrabi, cucumbers, zucchini, parsnips, peas and peppers, with lots of room left over for a complete assortment of herbs and an occasional oddity like popcorn, peanuts, watermelons or huckleberries.

In the beginning, we made the usual mistake of starting too big. In addition to the main garden, we rotated another garden behind the pigs and kept separate patches for berries, asparagus and rhubarb. It was a struggle to find enough manure and compost to fertilize it all. It was a bigger struggle to keep ahead of the weeds. The biggest struggle of all was coping with the glut. Visitors weren't allowed to leave without bags of fresh vegetables. We fed the pigs and the chickens on leftovers that fancy chefs would kill for. We sold what we could. We tried to give away zucchini to folks we'd barely met and were informed that they had spent the previous night leaving orphan baskets of their own zucchini on doorsteps around the village.

Eventually, we learned that a small, well-kept garden is less trouble than a too-large garden. And it can be even more productive. The berries and rhubarb and asparagus moved into the main garden, where we remember to weed in time. The pigpens we left for the pigs. We consolidated the orderly stuff and evicted the sprawling imperialists of the garden, like the pumpkins. (The pumpkins grow out of any old heap of organic rubbish and can sprawl all they want across the orchard or into the weeds.) For the most part, that sixth of an acre provides all the work and all the vegetables we can handle.

Any mention of appropriate garden size brings to mind a couple of transplanted urbanites we know who asked a neighbouring farmer to plough their first garden plot. It was immense – at least an acre. There were only the two of them, plus a couple of chronically feckless dogs.

"Why so . . . big?" we ventured politely, stifling all the adjectives that later came to mind.

Julie didn't answer. She just pointed across the garden to a mound of fresh, fine dirt that contrasted with the rough texture of the rest. I started to say "groundhog" but didn't get more than my mouth open before she hushed me.

Nodding toward the idiotic dogs, she whispered, "We're hoping the dogs will get used to Jerry and realize he won't harm them."

"Jerry? Who's Jerry?"

"The groundhog." She said this with a whiff of exasperation, as if I were the one sitting there with my tongue hanging out, looking for a lamppost.

"He's so cute when he sits up there turning his little head around."

"Maybe he's waiting for the plants to come up?"

"Yeh, like, that's why we made it so big. So there would be enough for all of us, including Jerry." She smiled. I was afraid she was going to start singing *Country Roads*. I was afraid I was going to be rude.

Instead, we merely wished her luck.

"Like, what do you mean, 'luck'?"

"Like, good luck training Jerry to refrain from eating those fresh, new sprouts as they come out of the ground. Just explain that if he waits a few months, until the garden is mature, there'll be plenty for everybody. I'm sure he'll understand."

If you keep the weeds, the deer and the groundhogs at bay, a small garden will suffice.

Meat can take up even less space. Rabbits are best housed in wire-bottomed cages. You can leave them in a shed or move the cages around the garden for portable fertilizer. Two or three does will provide enough offspring for rabbit dinner once a week. Care and feeding are light but regular chores: filling feed and water hoppers, checking for ear mites and minor ailments, introductions at breeding times. The hard part is the butchering.

Chickens are easier than rabbits. With a small, fenced yard, they can scratch up some of their own food and stay healthy with little fuss. Free-range chickens gather even more of their own food. Unfortunately, some of it will be from your garden – who wants to eat bugs when you can have a broccoli snack? And foxes are unduly fond of wandering hens. A fenced yard, say 25 by 25 feet, is just enough space for a dozen chickens to keep ahead of the weeds and safe from the foxes. If you want a labour-saving bonus, throw all the organic trash in the chicken yard: leaves, sawdust, cornstalks, anything too coarse for the compost pile goes into the chicken yard. They shred it, manure it and mix it with the soil. Whenever you need some rich potting soil or fill for the flowerbeds, scrape aside the new stuff and shovel out the rich compost from underneath. A dozen hens will give you all the fresh eggs you can eat, plus a seasonal glut for neighbourly gifts. After a couple of years, the layers taper off and can be stewed or pensioned off to make room for younger blood. With the addition of a single rooster to the flock, the hens will provide and raise their own replacements. That's all backyard stuff. It takes a few square feet for accommodation, a few dollars for feed and some simple equipment to dole out food and water in case you want to leave for a couple of days.

The work and the space requirements get more complex as the animals get bigger. Goats, pigs and cattle need more than the average backyard.

Goats are particularly delightful creatures. Only the adult males bring bad smells and nasty habits to the place. The ladies and kids are as clean and coquettish as anybody's house pets. You can house the breeding male downwind, or eliminate him altogether and take the ladies elsewhere to be bred. They enjoy a ride in the car, so a trip to the vet, to the breeder or to the butcher is much less complicated than with other animals. Our goats liked to ride in the passenger seat, with their front hooves propped on the dash.

Milking is a twice-a-day chore that demands serious time and attention. Meat goats, however, are a simpler matter (a meat goat is the same as a dairy goat—you just let the kids do the milking *au naturel*). You can raise a goat herd on a small acreage, but only with extremely good fences. They prefer apple trees, shrubs and flowers to the best pasture. And they prefer to be in any field other than the one you want them to be in. Katinka regularly mocked our efforts to fence her by walking along the top of the fence, tightrope fashion. Lots of time and trouble, but excellent food producers in a small space.

Pork is another ideal meat source for the mini-farm. And, in several respects, pigs are much less trouble than goats. You can buy weaners in June or July and have them ready for the freezer by November—no wintering-over problems. Better still, their appetites begin to surge in August and September, just when you're trying to get rid of the garden excess. A 25-pound summer weaner can weigh 250 pounds by fall, so two pigs are as many as most families can use. Unless you're Jack Semler, you'll need a stout box and a small truck to carry pigs to the vet or the butcher.

Jack had a full-grown pig, named Pig, who used to come to town with Jack in the Cadillac. Pig sat up in the front seat, just like Jack's date, and never ever disgraced herself. Pig was exceptional, though. She lived in the house and slept by the stove, a fact that led many in the district to blame Pig when Jack's house burned down. The story was that Pig upset the stove. Jack denied that, however, and insisted that Pig's only fault was a drinking problem. (I'm not making this up.) Anyway, Pig survived the fire only to die one bitterly cold night while out on a binge. She got into some fermenting apples (again) and was too drunk to find her way home. She either froze to death or died of pneumonia. One or the other. Jack has another pig now, but somehow it isn't the same. He makes this one ride in the backseat.

As Pig's sad tale makes clear, a wintered sow needs a warm shelter. Summer weaners are happy with an outdoor pen and any kind of makeshift shed that provides shade and shelter from autumn rains. If the pen is large enough, the pigs agree on a toilet corner and keep the rest spic-and-span. A good fence is essential, however. The smaller the space, the harder they try to escape. I've kept as many as five in a 50-by-50-foot pen of cedar rails and had no trouble. The same number in a smaller pen ate all the weeds and began to push at the fence for more. In the 50-by-50-foot pen, they were still finding fresh greens in October, and the flimsier fence was more than sufficient to hold them.

Cattle, on the other hand, are not well suited to the mini-farm. They need more grazing room (up to five acres per cow, depending on which expert you believe). They need hay to make it through one winter to maturity, and hay means machinery if you're producing your own. Fences have to be strong, and you'll need at least a half-ton truck to move them anywhere. Cattle, even a few, come pretty close to heavy-duty farming.

Fuel is one of the simplest needs that country dwellers can provide for themselves. Nearly every farm has some wood on it. If it's not a managed woodlot, it is at least a wild strip along ravines and rocky places that can't be ploughed. In fact, the poorer farms, those which are marginal for agriculture and thus cheap and attractive for country living, are the most likely places to find woodlands. They simply have more acreage that was too rough to plough and thus left to trees.

How many trees are enough depends, of course, on how drafty your house is and on how fast the trees grow. Like any other crop, forest growth varies according to soil fertility, rainfall, climate and good management.

Let's start with consumption. Larry Gay reckons that five or six cords of wood a year might be needed to heat a house in the northern United States. Here in eastern Ontario, we use four to five cords every winter for the house and a separate workshop. Five cords seems to be a rough, unscientific neighbourhood average. Those who are fussier about drafts and insulation get by on less.

Now production. Gay, starting with U.S. Forestry figures, concludes that "with a well-stocked average woodlot, you can count on about one cord per year from each acre." That would suggest that, in this neighbourhood, we need about five acres of forest to break even, cutting only as much as new growth would replace. That, however, would mean burning everything: saw logs, rotten logs and little top twigs. In practice, equilibrium in the woodlot requires a little more than an acre per cord. Taking five cords a year from 10 acres would leave enough flexibility for you to saw the best logs into lumber and leave the little limbs and rotters on the forest floor. It would still need management. You would have to select the culls for firewood, thinning crowded stands and taking out weed trees, dying trees and crooked and damaged trees. You'd have to fence out the cattle to let the undergrowth flourish (this is a woodlot, not a park). And you'd have to control the porcupines and beavers.

Now add it all up, and consider just how self-sufficient you want to be. A fraction of an acre is enough for a house, well, septic bed and a garden big enough for year-round fruit and vegetables. A backyard shed and a little pen can supply some meat and plenty of eggs. You can add room for flowers and landscaping and still keep the homestead down to an acre. Add a second acre if you want a pony, pigs, goats or a driving range. Five more acres of woodland will heat the house. Ten acres of woods will provide heat, plus some lumber and a little leeway on what you burn. That's 12 acres altogether, and this imaginary homestead is nearly self-sufficient. The rest – the beef, milk, coffee, salmon and so on – expand the homestead until it becomes an old-fashioned one-of-everything farm. This is the range of discretion that is the better part of value. We could become self-sufficient in salmon by buying a river in Scotland, or in coffee by buying a Colombian hillside. We might even become self-sufficient in tires by buying a Malaysian rubber plantation and Akron, Ohio, but that gets a little silly. Frankly, it's easier and cheaper to buy the tire.

A few acres can make us at least half self-sufficient. A thousand acres couldn't make us 100 percent self-sufficient, not with our modern tastes and habits. So a common rural choice is to grow a garden, cut some firewood and maybe keep a few hens or pets. Combined with cheaper rural housing, that's enough to cut the cost of living in half, with a minimum of simple chores. Much more than that becomes another job.

EARNING A LIVING

▼▼▼▼▼

Okay, so the city hasn't proved to be as exciting as it promised to be. And country places aren't as dull and distant as fiction paints them. Then there's the money – so much less of it is needed to live in country places. Why, then, are the cities still filling up? Why, especially, are the cities filling up when the numbers show that most of us would really prefer not to live in the city?

The answer, for many, has been "the job" – the great kink in the bowel of modern life. In the city, there's been a sense that the countryside is some vast sea of unemployment, where career opportunities are limited to farming or pumping gas, where not much happens and where there's no way to get ahead. That has been true in the past. It is still true in some places. And it may always be true for some people. But the fact is that the job economy has gone through some wrenching changes in recent years and appears to be on the brink of even greater changes. Those changes amount to a revolution in the way we work, where we work, whom we work for and how we get ahead.

Let's look first at the big changes, then consider the implications for earning a living outside the city.

BIG CHANGES

Cities and suburbs and the social geography haven't happened as the simple result of human choices. Mrs. Cro-Magnon didn't say, "I'm sick of this drafty old cave, Gronk. Let's move to Cleveland." It just didn't happen that way.

The shape of settlement has, instead, been a creature of economy. For millions of years, there were no cities. That was not because elevators hadn't been invented yet. It was because nearly every Tom, Dick and Jane in the human race was too busy gathering food to have time for much else. There was no surplus population to fill the bars and malls and no one willing to feed such a surplus without an economic quid pro quo.

By the time Rome flowered, three-quarters of the world's population was still working in the food economy. In other words, it required three people tilling the land in order to feed four mouths. That 25 percent of the population not needed down on the farm was, by then, free to live in the city, to govern, soldier, spout philosophy or just hang around the forum.

It was, in other words, pivotal developments in the technology and economy of food production that made the city possible. Further such developments allowed the cities to grow to proportions that could not have been imagined by the first food gatherers. By 1940, just 18 percent of the work force in the United States kept the country fed, with a surplus for export. By 1960, only 9 percent of the American work force was still on the farm. Now, 3 percent of Americans feed the country and export a surplus. In Canada, 4 percent feed the rest and then some.

In the pivotal period between 1905 and 1915, American agriculture dropped from being the largest sector of the labour force to being the smallest. Manufacturing and service sectors boomed while the farm sector shrank. North America didn't eat any less. It simply produced more food with fewer people. We might regret the decline of the family farm for lots of reasons, but declining production isn't one of them.

Now it appears that the manufacture of things is in the throes of the same kind of revolution that overturned the food economy. Until just before World War I, the most common occupation in America was "farmer." Then "farmer" gave way to "labourer." By 1979, "labourer" had yielded to "clerk." The industrial changes are as vital to the social geography as the agricultural changes were. If agricultural technology made the city possible, the industrial revolution made it necessary. The mass production of things was a creature of the city, and vice versa. Industry and the city grew in tandem. The question is whether they will shrink in tandem.

Historically, industry needed four key ingredients in order to flourish: transportation to bring the raw materials together, capital to build the factories, a labour pool large enough to staff the factories, and a market to buy the goods. The city served all those needs.

Transportation was the first key to the city. Early cities were spawned where the most vital roads crossed, where people and goods could move most easily. But the raw materials of the industrial era added another element – bulk. Coal, cotton, ore and timber were characterized by their great volume or mass in proportion to their value. So transportation had to be cheap as well as plentiful. That meant waterways to bring materials from abroad and, later, railways to reach the inland areas cheaply. It was no accident that the booming industrial cities sat smack on the interface between sea transport and easy access to a well-populated hinterland.

The capital to buy the tools and build the factories came from investors and banks centred in the city. The social contacts, business meetings and contracts that arranged the capital happened face-to-face. The movers and shakers had to be in the same place.

The labour component of the industrial equation was most easily mustered in the city. Only in the city was the concentration of labour dense enough to fill a large factory. When everyone had to walk to work, that dense concentration was essential to get them all to the mill on time. Moreover, the poverty and rootlessness of the city actually enhanced the labour supply by keeping labour cheap and dependent; few could afford to say "to heck with this" and go off to do something else for a while. The poor, teeming Dickensian slum was, at the time, the solution to an industrial problem and a fixture of that economic structure.

The market, too, was well served by an urban concentration. Goods might be sold within the city or, at worst, exported via the same transportation system that had brought the raw material to the centre. The denser the population, the cheaper the distribution costs.

City and industry grew in a kind of symbiotic relationship. Each made the other possible. Each made the other necessary. And each thrived on the growth of the other. So tight was the fit between the two that the mutual benefits of size became ingrained in modern thought. The central myth of the industrial mind remains riveted on the mass production of things, long after the economic reality has changed to decentralized services.

Present-day Babbitts continue their obsession with growth for its own sake. One cool April night in 1988, an Ontario township council faced an angry group of ratepayers who objected to another housing development in the midst of an established neighbourhood. The ratepayers' spokesperson, a dignified and articulate investment broker, pointed out that the new development would mean higher taxes for everyone for the installation of extra services, roads and streetlights. No small community has ever expanded and then cut taxes. Bigger communities pay more.

"Yes," the deputy reeve conceded, "but we have to keep growing." It hung there in the evening air like the eleventh commandment. Nobody asked why they had to keep growing.

The anger fizzled, and the petitioners left the chamber defeated and deflated. The growth myth was too ingrained to question. The deputy reeve's hex could as easily have been "jobs" or "GNP" or a veiled allusion to the fact that a neighbouring township might be growing faster. Local councils tend to watch fretfully over their shoulders as rural townships cross out the population scores on the townline sign and chalk in higher numbers. Industrial growth and population. They are the municipal equivalent of machismo.

APPEARANCE AND REALITY

If the myth hasn't changed much, the reality has. The reality is that the making of things has given way to the provision of services. The old mass-production factory – the one that fattened on economies of scale and urban growth – is gone. It's gone to China and India and Brazil. It's gone just as surely as the family farm. Look at the numbers.

By 1986, there were barely two million manufacturing jobs left in Canada. That represents a mere 17 percent of the work force. In the five years from 1981 to 1986, manufacturing jobs fell by 5 percent. Overall employment, in the same period, grew by almost 6 percent. American figures show the same trends. The economy has more goods, more jobs and more money than it has ever had before. But the manufacturing employment sector is on the same slippery slope as the old agricultural sector. Meanwhile, the ghost of the industrial past continues to push the myths of concentration, density and the old rationale for cities.

Even that core of industry which remains is a very different creature. Henry Ford wouldn't recognize a modern auto plant. Automation, robotics and the microchip have changed the whole relationship between jobs and production. Fewer workers produce far more. Computers can manage the process so minutely that smaller and smaller production runs are not only feasible, they are becoming the rule. Ford couldn't even alter the colour of his Model T – any colour you want as long as it's black – but today, you can name the colour, number of doors, engine size and any permutation of scores of optional extras. The microchips will order up the right components to assemble that "custom" car anywhere in the production run. The assembly line doesn't even slow down to make the change.

Clothing, chemical, electronic and aeronautic industries all have the technology to produce small custom runs just as easily as the technology of the past industrial era managed mass production. Using cheap and simple keyboard commands, a printer can alter a publication to suit special groups of readers and regional audiences. Even the U.S. military, whose budget dwarfs that of most countries, buys 78 percent of its goods in lots of under 100 items.

The changing technology of production carries two essential messages for anyone interested in earning a living. First, it takes fewer and fewer people to produce the same number of goods. Secondly, goods can be produced economically in smaller and smaller batches. Put those trends together – high productivity and shorter production runs – and the old need to concentrate a mass labour force begins to disappear. Magna International, the recent giant of the auto-parts business, restricts its factories to 100 employees. When they grow larger than that, Magna divides the work and starts a new factory in another location.

So much for the concentration of labour.

Consider capital. The major world stock markets, money markets, futures and commodity markets trade by satellite. It takes milliseconds to move money from Kuwait to Flin Flon, Manitoba. The movers and shakers can dial direct to one another anywhere in the world. If and when they must meet face-to-face, they are a day's flight away from anywhere. It's absurd to even think about the concentration of investment capital in any particular city. Money isn't bags of gold anymore; it's keyed entries in electronic accounts. The symbols (Bay Street, Wall Street and the clubs of St. James) are still at their old city addresses. But the money is global, and it moves instantly to wherever the prospects of profit are greatest.

Raw materials and transport? The key to the first cities? They're still important, but only as important as the production of goods. Remember that barely 17 percent of the work force is still involved in that kind of manufacturing. Most jobs are now in the service sector. We type, process insurance claims, sell, advise, fix teeth, teach and do a jillion other things that don't need a barge load of raw material delivered to the workplace every morning. And the products of our labour can be delivered to a distant customer by modem or mail.

The transportation network is no less important than it ever was, but it's different. Back in the old days, when cities were essential, we shipped materials with great bulk and low unit value (like lumps of coal). Now, we transport words by telephone, pictures by fax, energy by wire. The bulk is smaller, the unit value of the shipments higher. Such a change means that the network can be faster, simpler and more diverse. It is simple and cheap to string a telephone wire to a small service industry in the country. It would not be feasible to dig a canal or build a railway to a small country steel mill. The nature and scale of industry have changed, and the need for transportation has changed with them. The city is no longer the essential hub for railways and canals that it once was.

Finally, there's the market. For the goods market, the buying and selling of things, distribution would indeed be simpler if all the customers were concentrated in a single spot. All other things being equal, the cost of distribution should fall. But all other things aren't equal. To begin with, consumers aren't willing to live in a heap. Even in the city, they're scattered across miles and miles of urban geography. Delivery within a city, given urban traffic and parking problems, may be more expensive than shipping goods out of town. The biggest difference, however, comes back to real estate costs. City rents and taxes make urban distribution points expensive to run, higher volumes notwithstanding. Don't believe it? Look around your own city. Where are the high-bulk consumer outlets, the auto dealers, lumberyards, furniture and appliance showrooms? In the centre of the city or out on the fringe? Then, the next time you buy a car or a load of lumber, take your best city price to a small-town dealer, and ask if he can beat the city price. He can.

As the economy continues to shift away from the production of things and into the provision of services, the economic raison d'être of the big industrial city fades away. The economy doesn't need a hub of railways and canals. It doesn't need a huge pool of concentrated labour. It doesn't need a specific place for the face-to-face arrangement of capital. And the advantages of market concentration are lost as the cities become too expensive for the sellers. Even the former advantage of advertising in concentrated markets has lost its economic legs. A native trapper in northern Saskatchewan comes out of the bush and turns on the local news from Chicago or 24 other American cities. What market concentration?

The major industrial centres have grown so large that they've begun to touch one another at the edges. Picture the landscape bounded by Chicago, Toronto, Boston and New York. Where is the epicentre of that industrial sprawl? An industrialist almost anywhere in that web ships, receives and communicates throughout the area. The need for concentration in any one spot begins to look sillier even as the cities grow.

I have a friend who owns a bookbinding business serving customers from coast to coast. A big chunk of the business was divided between Toronto and Montreal. Keeping the company in either centre met only one small part of the shipping problem, and my friend was still stuck with the high cost of operating in the city. He moved the company lock, stock and binder to a small town situated on road and railway lines halfway between the two centres.

Will the cities die as the industrial economy deserts them? Certainly not. Any concentration of people will generate services. Somebody has to sell hamburgers and insurance to all those urbanites. Somebody has to fix their cars and drive their buses. But the industrial necessity is gone. The city won't die, but it's no longer necessary.

The self-appointed urban elite will continue to demand feeding and attention long after the economic raison d'être has left town. That, however, will result in a new kind of city. Not an economic city, but one that thrives solely by virtue of its political clout.

FIRST-ONE-IN SYNDROME

So, if the city is no longer necessary and if high real estate prices and wages make urban industry more costly, why hasn't more industry moved?

First, let's consider that trickle of manufacturing that has already left for the country. It's a movement that's hard to see. Because industry can now work economically in smaller units, movement away from cities is possible. And yet, ironically, because that movement occurs in small units, it is harder to see. The organs that extend our vision (like television) show big things, city things. Changes that develop with small movements aren't dramatic enough to make the news. That doesn't mean they aren't happening. If a big-city steel plant decamps to a country town, that's news. If they set up a small, new plant to stamp out door panels in the country and gradually let the city mill wither, that's not news. But that's what's happening. The city will be the last to know.

The movement is further obscured by the much larger moves abroad and the dramatic shrinkage in the overall manufacturing sector. If a thousand steel-mill jobs are moved to Brazil or replaced by new technology, then the much smaller shift of 50 jobs to a country town is barely noticed.

Even in the countryside, the shift of manufacturing jobs from the city has not had a dramatic impact on employment. In many such instances, it has merely absorbed those workers who are no longer needed by the mines, forests and farms. New employers replace old employers, and the net change is usually small.

The perspective on this trend is also made fuzzy by the move in the opposite direction on the other side of the boardroom. As production breaks down into smaller units and moves to low-wage, low-rent districts, here or abroad, the ownership of that production becomes more centralized than ever. Decentralized production, centralized ownership. The news is takeover and amalgamation at the top, rather than the new diversity at the production level.

That dichotomy – the simultaneous centralization and decentralization of industry – will have its own consequences. We might guess, for example, that centralized ownership will result in the greater bureaucratization of industry as the takeover artists try to cope with the much greater problem of running the empires they've assembled. Or it might result in the diminution of national political controls as the growing conglomerates use their power to move capital around the globe unhindered. Whatever happens, centralized ownership will not affect that opposite move toward the decentralization of production and jobs. It is the control over capital that is being centralized – not centralized in a few cities but centralized in a few hands. The factories, what are left of them, will take advantage of the new technology to diversify, divide and move to wherever rents, wages and distribution costs are most favourable.

In 1988, the Hershey Chocolate Company, a large multinational conglomerate with its headquarters in Hershey, Pennsylvania (population 7,407), bought a part of Planters Peanuts. The takeover included a peanut-packing plant in Toronto (population 3,500,000). The peanut plant employed about 100 people in an ageing downtown building that promised to be expensive to keep and more expensive to fix. Hershey decided to move the peanut operation from expensive Toronto to cheaper Smiths Falls (population 9,000), where they already had a branch-plant chocolate factory. The sequence is typical of the kind of move we're talking about. Look at the elements: large multinational company, growing through takeovers and amalgamation; centralized ownership; decentralized production in smaller, widely scattered plants; a preference for cheap rural locations rather than expensive urban ones.

What happened to the 100 workers? The company offered to move them from Toronto, the most expensive city in Canada, to Smiths Falls, where they could have new homes at less than a third of Toronto prices and within an easy walk of the plant. The plant, in a parklike setting, is a stroll away from shopping, athletic fields, boating, curling, squash, tennis, and much more. A few senior staff members accepted the offer, but most of the production staff refused. A hundred new jobs opened up in Smiths Falls, and a hundred jobs disappeared in Toronto. A hundred jobs are significant in Smiths Falls, barely noticeable in Toronto. As far as the national media were concerned, the move wasn't big enough to be seen. What trend?

Why wouldn't the workers take advantage of cheaper living, less commuting and a big cash difference in home equity? What kept them in Toronto? Undeniably, many had strong family and personal ties to consider. But according to one employee, it was also fear of layoffs. They felt they could lose a job in Toronto and find another. In Smiths Falls, who knows? What if they got laid off at the peanut plant? Where could they find another job in a little place like that? That's the myth of urban opportunity talking. And the old myth of the rural economy – farmers and gas-pump attendants.

In reality, the peanut packers might have fallen back on Stanley Tools, Westinghouse, Jergens and a dozen others within 15 minutes of the new peanut plant – all large multinationals with small, decentralized, rural plants, moving away from high urban costs and congestion. And that's just the industrial sector, the diminishing corner of the economy that has already given way to the much more portable service sector.

What's happening in the service sector that matters for anyone contemplating a move? Two things. First, there is the fact that most of the service sector follows the customers. A given population can only support so many lawyers, hairdressers, dentists, waitresses, consultants and insurance salesmen. These occupations don't lead demographic trends, they follow them. As an area grows, the opportunities for service-sector employment grow with it. Unlike industrial jobs, which depend on some distant and centralized ownership to decide things like plant closings, the service sector tends to enjoy more local control and less arbitrary layoff patterns. In the service sector, if the customers are there, the business is there and the jobs are there. If, on the other hand, it's an industrial job you're counting on, the plant can have lots of business and still decide to lay off the staff and move the whole operation to Brazil.

The second consideration in the service sector is the trend that hasn't really happened – not yet, anyway. I'm talking about the modern scions of the ancient tradition of cottage industry, the start-at-home businesses that were supposed to burgeon again as the personal computer made it possible to link your brain to a customer or office anywhere in the world. Alvin Toffler called it the "electronic cottage" and cited the prospect as the linchpin of *The Third Wave*. That was in 1980. And despite the fact that the technology is better and cheaper than ever, the wave hasn't swamped the beach. There are lots of work-at-home opportunities but not as much action as Toffler predicted.

John Naisbitt, author of *Megatrends*, argues that the electronic cottage fizzled because people really prefer to go to the office, where they have somebody to talk to at coffee break and no cats walking across the keyboard.

Others, like Mohammad Qadeer, professor of urban and regional planning at Queen's University at Kingston, Ontario, see evidence that the electronic cottage is happening but that the work is being farmed out to Singapore and Hong Kong rather than to some programmer's idyllic setting in the hills of Vermont.

The failure of the third wave to break might also be blamed on the first-one-in syndrome. It's human nature. You see a thousand people on the beach and no one in the lake, and you assume the water is cold. One eccentric breaks away to make a decent living at home, while a thousand stick to city commuting, and you assume that there must be a catch. Ditching office politics and rush hour for a workday that begins on the patio sounds so attractive, you assume if it were really that easy, everybody would be doing it.

Whatever the current numbers say, the changes that set the stage for the electronic cottage are still in play. More than ever, it is possible to do business in smaller and smaller units. And more than ever, it is possible to do business at any distance. More than ever, it is possible to do urban jobs in the country.

Norma runs a desk-top publishing company from her rural home, the same little house she grew up in. It isn't near much, certainly not any city or publishing mecca. The business is a cramped room, an off-the-shelf personal computer and whatever time Norma can spare from mothering three small children. She sets copy and simple graphics for advertising circulars and throwaway weeklies, the kind of work that used to be done by a big Linotype machine, a skilled operator, a graphic artist, a layout artist and a big, noisy, mechanical composing room. Norma's output is a simple disc. She can hand-deliver it in the family car to a printing plant nearby or mail it to a city printer or put it on the modem and send it anywhere in the world.

Norma is a classic electronic-cottage operator. Toffler says she's the wave of the future. Naisbitt says she'd rather be at the office. Qadeer says she's being outbid by the Third World cottages. Norma says she's quite happy where she is.

IMPLICATIONS FOR CAREER

Years ago, little blond, blue-eyed Ewan announced that he wanted to be an Indian when he grew up. His parents liked that idea a lot better than other careers he might have chosen, and so, regardless of how impractical it might have seemed, they gave him no reason to alter his ambition.

Then he came home from grade eight with a long accordion of computer pages, the result of something called "career day." When we were that age, it was called "What do you want to be when you grow up?" It didn't, however, take a whole day, and because it wasn't done on computers, nobody took it very seriously. Now, with official pleats and holes down the side, it all looks so scientific that we have to take it seriously: astronomer, chemist, how many degrees at what level to do this, that or the other. In reality, it still doesn't mean much more than wanting to be an Indian.

At his age, Ewan still believes that chemists spend their days in bubbling labs, making vile smells and the odd explosion. He'll learn. And he'll want to be at least three other things before he finishes school. Given the accelerated changes in the labour market, he'll need at least three more careers to carry him through to a pensionable age.

To put it simply, the day of the 40-year career is dead. Even those few professions which, like sharks and cockroaches, are enduring enough to survive the apocalypse won't last a decade without changes so profound that retraining will be essential. Lawyers now search for precedents electronically. Dentists coat teeth to prevent the cavities they used to fill. Doctors test for things they used to feel for. And chemists spend more time with computer models than with bubbling tubes of smelly stuff.

Those who survive the changes may not be those who latch onto a big corporate ladder and assume they'll spend the next 40 years on a straight, upward path. Too many workers have suffered layoffs to go on entrusting lifetime security to corporate paternalism. Those who survive will be those who can adapt, learn and move with the changes. As industry divides itself into smaller production units, survivors will learn to work in smaller groups. As jobs follow capital to cheaper places, survivors will discard any bias against rural areas. In many industries, the top is no longer at the centre. The top of the Johns-Manville ladder is in Douglas County, Colorado. For Xerox, it's Webster, New York. In those companies, in order to rise to the top, you have to live in smaller places. In those companies, New York, Paris, Tokyo and Toronto are the promotional backwaters.

In many careers, leaving the city can put a temporary cap on career ambitions. In banking, insurance or the civil service, for example, the hierarchy ends in the city. If you want to be president of the Toronto Dominion Bank, then sooner or later you'll have to live in Toronto. That's true if you plan to spend your entire career within a single hierarchy, if your employer promotes from within and does not recruit experience from outside and if you have access to that linear promotion ladder.

In some careers, however, the most rapid rise to the top results from lateral "stream hopping." The aspiring executive gains experience by moving sideways through a variety of positions. Though he may never gain many promotions within any single hierarchy, each shift is to a higher rung on somebody else's ladder. Movement is rapid, since the stream hopper never has to wait for the fossils above him to die or retire. And the rise is, in part, assured through the sheer variety of experience obtained. In such a pattern, jobs in smaller centres may be an advantage. In the country, where specialists are an unaffordable luxury, the relatively inexperienced are expected to take on a wider variety of tasks.

Ralph, an ambitious newcomer to law enforcement, took a chance on accepting an initial posting to a remote northern community. In his two years there, he handled murder cases, drugs, a train robbery and assorted other criminal investigations. He not only caught the crooks but did the detective work and fought each case through the courts and appeals. Two years later, he returned to the densely settled south and was amazed to find his fellow police-academy graduates still writing speeding tickets and doing little else. There, he discovered, head office had specialists for all the difficult cases, and the ambitious beginners had years to wait before they would be allowed to get their hands on the kind of work that Ralph did every day in the north.

Doctors tell a similar tale. When the community is too small for specialists, the ambitious generalist does it all and gains experience that his urban colleagues never have a chance to acquire.

The prospect for good exurban careers can be hard to see, especially for those accustomed to looking at the world from the middle of a crowd. Recently, I shared a booth at a Picton café with a youngish Toronto-executive type. Mike is a pleasant, serious man with a wife and baby daughter back in the city. They're about to build a new family home, and Mike has just paid $265,000 for the lot. A patch of Metro just 40 feet wide, and he's in for a quarter of a million before he starts to build!

"I wonder what land's worth around here?" he asked, just a little wistfully. Picton is a pretty town of about 4,000 people. The sailing harbour is a five-minute walk from the centre of town. Homes are well kept. There's a good French restaurant just out of town and a large provincial park along the lakeshore. Toronto is a two-hour drive for those who feel the need.

He speculated for a while on just how big a mansion he might have in Picton for the price of his petunia bed in Toronto, and then he shook his head.

"But where on earth would people work around here?" he said. It wasn't a question. It was his dismissal of a pleasant speculation.

"Mike, you can't be serious! There are bankers, doctors, dentists, art dealers, accountants and even real estate agents here." Mike is in real estate. "Your own company has an office here, for God's sake."

"Sure," he agreed. "But there's never any turnover in places like this. Here, or in London, Ontario, or in any of the small, pretty places, we have jobs but few vacancies. In the Toronto office, people come and go so fast that there are always openings. Here, we hire people or transfer them from Toronto, and they never want to leave."

Somehow, Mike and I saw the same set of facts and came to different conclusions. He concluded that the number of job openings here are too few, and I left the café thinking that Picton must be a damned nice place to live if nobody wants to leave. And somehow, the people who live here seem to manage careers just fine.

Studies show that places like Picton actually provide more jobs than their residents fill. In fact, there are 106 jobs for every 100 working residents of the average small Canadian town. Commuters from the surrounding countryside take the extra jobs. Far from being the desert of unemployment that Mike imagines, the typical small town creates more jobs than it needs.

Mike was right about one thing, though. The people who live in places like Picton don't have a thousand job vacancies a month to choose from. For most of us, fortunately, one is enough. We might not make enough to afford a $265,000 petunia bed, but we somehow manage to scrape by. We even have room for a few petunias.

GETTING A JOB IN THE COUNTRY

The job hunt proceeds the same way in the country as it does in the city. Except that there are those, like Mike, who imagine that it's somehow different where job seekers and openings number in the dozens rather than the thousands.

For people like Mike, who already have careers in a widely scattered industry, the easiest way to move is a simple job transfer. For the prettiest places, you might have to wait. But a move, when it comes, is not a big career disruption. In banking, real estate, insurance, government and retail chains, transfers are daily fare.

In those jobs, it might even be possible to arrange a trial run, a temporary assignment to fill in, consult or help out in a local pinch. Use the time to look around, see if you like the place, and scout out other local jobs.

If the employer isn't widely dispersed, many occupations are. Nurses, teachers, computer types, salespeople, doctors, lawyers, accountants and anyone who can repair anything can move those skills to just about anywhere they decide to live.

The gas-pump-and-farmer myth falls apart completely when you look at the real distribution of occupations. Hodge and Qadeer conclude that small towns and big cities are virtually indistinguishable when you look at the kinds of jobs available in which places. With the understandable exception of the farm, communities of all sizes show almost the same mix of jobs in manufacturing, construction, transportation and communications, personal service, public administration, and so on. Mining jobs are concentrated in small one-industry towns, and agricultural employment is more limited in the cities. Otherwise, the mix is nearly constant, no matter how large or small the community.

So far, we've talked about working for others. For many, however, a move to the country opens up new prospects for self-employment. Why new prospects? Why should a country environment be any more conducive to small enterprise than an urban environment, where markets are bigger? There are three reasons, and all of them stem directly from the fact that everything (including the market) is on a smaller scale.

First, smaller markets mean that big business isn't all that interested. The field is more open to small business. Sure, Texaco is going to have a gas station there, the bank will be a branch of a big chain, and a fast-food chain won't be far behind. But that still leaves lots of unfilled niches in the smaller marketplace. Norma can open her little desk-top business in the spare room behind the stairs because there isn't much competition at that end of the market. The big printing plant down the road does much the same mix of typesetting, graphics and layout that Norma offers, but they're more interested in the big jobs. They're quite content to let Norma handle the small circulars and one-off flyers. The same division of the market happens in the city, but there, a hundred Normas compete for the scraps.

Secondly, opening a new business on the smallest scale means less capital needed at the start. That's particularly true in the country, where business space is so much cheaper than it is in the city. A smaller investment makes it easier to get into (and out of) a business. It's not such a huge commitment for a neophyte.

Finally, the new country business is so readily visible that introduction is not the problem it is in the city. There is no advertising campaign or long wait in the Yellow Pages before customers learn where you are and what you do. My new neighbour started a business this spring. He moved in and hung a hand-painted sign on the fence. The sign says, "Pedro's Welding and General Repair." An arrow points to his house and the workshop in an attached garage.

Now it happened that I had a garden sickle with a crack in the handle. A new weld might be cheaper than a new sickle, I thought. So I dropped in to see the new neighbour. A tall, bearded man in coveralls was grinding something in the garage.

"Are you Pedro?" I asked.

"Yah," he shouted, over the grinder.

Yah? Pedro? "Can you fix this?" I asked him, handing over the broken sickle. The grinder chattered to a halt while he turned the tool over in his hands and then held it up close to his bright blue eyes.

"Yah, shore, das es easy," he said, in an accent so German that there couldn't be any mistake.

"Where did you get a name like Pedro?" I asked.

"Mozambique. I come here from Afrique. Dere dey calling me

Pedro. Name es Peter, so dey calling me Pedro."

Our little country road, you should know, is not really on the way from Mozambique. It's not even a main route to the general store, three miles away. Naturally, I got a little curious. Pedro, or Peter as it turns out, is actually Swiss German via Mozambique and ended up here on the way to visit Swiss friends on the other side of the lake. He liked the area, saw the house, bought it and opened his business. Just like that. He was going to call it "Peter's," but there were already a couple of Peters in business around here. So "Pedro" was his concession to the competition.

I'm wondering how a man with no introductions and 20 words of English manages in this unilingual, conservative community, on a road so quiet that the white dog who sleeps all night on the pavement is eight years old and has never been hit by a car. And all Peter/Pedro does is buy a house and hang his sign on the fence.

"So how's business?" I ask.

"I lack it here yus fine," he says. "Very nice place."

"The business?" I try it a little louder. "Lots of customers?"

"Oh, business! Yah, business es goot." And looking around, it's hard to argue. There's business all over the shop and spilling out onto the drive.

Later that same day, I ran into Doug, a one-man construction company from the village. He mentioned some broken equipment, and I mentioned Peter/Pedro, who, incidentally, did a first-class job on the sickle and didn't charge a dime. I thought I'd return the favour.

"Oh, him," says Doug. "Yeh, he's working on a job for me right now. Fine welder, but you can't understand a word he says."

Try opening a successful one-man business in the city that quickly when your entire communication with the market is a hand-lettered sign on the fence.

A University of California study suggests that a similar blossoming of rural enterprise is happening in parts of the United States. In a close look at urban migrants to three rural California counties, the researchers found that almost 4 out of every 10 employed newcomers began businesses. More than half of those starting new businesses said they decided to do so after moving to the country.

Others decide on a business and then go looking for the right community. Richard and Rosemary wanted to open a bookstore; they just didn't know where. So they took a list of Ontario towns, set out in order of size, then matched that list with a list of established bookstores and scratched out every town that already had one. They moved to the biggest town (population 9,000) that didn't already have a bookstore. Now they have stores in three small towns. They've built their success on going to places where there was no competition. Small places.

WHAT'S IT LIKE?

It's possible, then, to earn a living in smaller places. But what's it really like? What about getting to work? And salaries?

My city friends tell me that they like the convenience of the city, the convenience of being close to work and close to everything else. Commuting, they say, would spoil any advantages of country life.

Personally, I work about 10 feet from my bed or out on the patio when the weather's nice. So I can't make a solid refutation of the commuter objection without sounding smug. What about my fellow exurbanites, though? Do they drive great distances to the job? Not according to the numbers.

Hodge and Qadeer studied Canadian towns and villages with populations below 10,000. There, 71 percent of the labour force work in the communities where they live. In a town of 10,000, that's walking distance or a very short drive. The other 29 percent commute. The commuters travel an average of 22.4 miles. If that drive takes 30 minutes, it would be comparable to the time spent on the road by the average urban commuter.

The myth of urban convenience versus long-distance rural commuting led to predictions that the energy crunch of the 1970s would bring exurbanites back to the city. It didn't happen. It didn't happen because jobs, like people, have been scattered over wide areas. And getting from the country to the job doesn't necessarily take more gas than getting from the city to the job. Not anymore.

Nor is superior urban public transport much of a saving when you consider how little it's used. U.S. Census Bureau studies show that only about 6 percent of the U.S. work force uses public transport to get to work. That 1980 figure represents a decline of about one-third from 1970. Ironically, the decade that brought the energy crisis showed an increase in the use of the car and a decline in the use of public transportation. It's not a simple trend, and it's complicated by other factors, such as the quality of public transportation; but commuting patterns must be related to the fact that, by 1980, the majority of American workers were "lateral commuters," living in one suburb or fringe community and working in another.

The view of the city as a centre does not hold. Few can afford to live downtown. Fewer still can live as well as work downtown. The reality is that jobs have scattered over a broader area and workers must move with the jobs or commute. The reality is that city workers may actually commute far more than workers from small towns and country places. The typical rural dweller does not drive a great distance to a city job. The typical urbanite, however, does indeed drive to a job in the distant urban fringe.

What about salaries? Isn't the city the place where every farm boy goes to make his fortune? Aren't salaries, at least, better in the city? Yes and no. Yes, the city has more than its share of television stars, professional athletes and high-rolling capitalist kings. Those people make lots of money. And on the average, urban incomes are higher. That's the bad news.

The good news is that the gap is closing and that when the cost of living is accounted for, the gap opens the other way.

Individual income distribution looked like this in 1986:

Size of Area Population	Canada	Ontario	British Columbia
All areas	$18,746	$20,203	$19,198
100,000 plus	20,232	21,364	19,910
30,000-100,000	17,845	18,513	18,337
Under 30,000	16,931	17,921	18,480
Rural	15,639	17,340	17,669

Rural incomes are, indeed, just 83 percent of the Canadian average of $18,746. But look what's happening in Ontario and British Columbia, two provinces where the pressures of the city are forcing some employers out into the small towns and rural places. In Ontario, rural incomes are 92 percent of the Canadian average and 81 percent of booming metropolitan incomes. In British Columbia, rural incomes are just 6 percent below the average and 11 percent below big urban incomes.

The rural average is distorted, to some extent, by low farm incomes. Let's look at the incomes in small towns, those with fewer than 30,000 people. The national gap between small towns and all the rest is just 10 percent. In Ontario, it shrinks to 4 percent, and in British Columbia to 2 percent. An income in small-town British Columbia is just $266 a year less than the mostly urban Canadian average. That's not a big gap. That's not even close to the myth of city streets paved with gold, where country boys go to make their fortunes.

Now look at the other side of the financial equation. Look at the cost of living. Look, especially, at housing. In Parry Sound, Haliburton, Barry's Bay, Green Valley and scores of other communities, you can buy a three-bedroom brick house on a serviced lot in town for about $75,000. A comparable house in Toronto might cost $200,000 to $300,000, depending on the neighbourhood. If the difference is $150,000 and if interest rates are 10 percent, then housing alone will cost $15,000 a year more in the city. The wage gap, however, is a little more than $3,000. In other words, you could earn $3,000 more in the city but pay $15,000 a year more for a house. A net loss of $12,000 a year!

Yes, incomes are higher in the city. And, no, it's not worth it.

TRANSITION STRATEGIES

▼▼▼▼▼

There are those who plunge into icy waters and those who wade in slowly, a cautious hand on the dock just in case, at any moment, dry might seem a better place to be.

So, too, with moving house. The cautious inch out into the suburbs, while others, in a fit of geographic passion, leap headlong into rural seas. Take your pick.

For most, the style of making a move is closely tied to career. If you're a nurse, you can live and work just about anywhere you choose. If, on the other hand, you're determined to be a streetcar conductor, then moving is only possible within commuting range of the city. The alternative is to abandon both city and job simultaneously, and that can be an icy plunge.

Between the extremes are smaller steps that allow the cautious to leave the city without burning all their bridges. Let's look first at a few options for the long-distance career: commuting, flexible working time, moving the job, freelance work and leave of absence. Each such tactic permits the mover to keep a toehold on the city career until new country roots have taken.

JOB TRANSITIONS

Ray is a cartographer who drives 60 miles to work each day and 60 miles home. That's about twice the usual range for commuters. Ray insists he enjoys the drive, and he takes passengers to help defray the cost. Sixty miles out of the city, Ray has a large yard, big enough for grass and a mini-forest of shade trees. The girls have a playhouse of their own. They can walk to the lake, to the store and to church. It's a nice place to live, but there really isn't a big call for cartographers in the neighbourhood. Ray has to give up cartography, give up the country, or drive. He drives.

For many, a partial solution is to adjust the hours on the job. Some municipalities have encouraged employers to adopt "flex-time" schedules, which allow workers to shift their coming and going times. The city benefits from the reduction in traffic congestion at peak hours. The workers benefit from work hours that suit their personal lives: the night owls can sleep in and work late; early birds can beat the morning rush and come home in the afternoon; parents can split their schedules so that one or the other of them can meet the kids after school; commuters can speed up their trip to the workplace by avoiding peak hours and spending less time in traffic jams.

The big break for long-distance commuters comes when the flexibility in work time allows fewer working days. Squeezing the 40-hour week into three or four days is a boon. Although the days are longer, the number of trips to the city are fewer. A four-day week would give Ray an extra 2½ hours of spare time, plus the gas saved by making one less trip.

Moving the old job to a new address can be an even better solution. Doug sold industrial equipment in Toronto. His cottage was 200 miles away. His dream was to retire to the cottage as early as possible. It wasn't quite as simple as packing and moving, however. For starters, the family had never spent a winter at the lake before. They weren't at all sure it would be the same relaxing idyll in January that it was in July. Then there was the small matter of earning a living. The family needed a trial period, some transition between what they knew was adequate and what they thought might be terrific.

They began with a move to the cottage and a cut in Doug's working time. He squeezed his sales calls into a few days a week and commuted from the lake to Toronto. Same job, but fewer hours and a lot more driving. If things didn't work out, going back was a simple matter of readjusting his time to the old schedule.

When they had survived one winter at the lake and discovered that the rural world didn't end on Labour Day, Doug pushed the transition one more notch. He swapped his Toronto sales territory for another one closer to the cottage. Same company, same career, but no more driving back and forth to the city.

The next step, I expect, will come when Doug discovers that life in the cottage by the lake is so much cheaper than in the city that his early retirement can take its course and he can quit driving to work at all.

Jim, a city photographer, took a similar route. He and his wife Sandra finally moved 70 miles out, to the tiny village of Middleville. Middleville, of course, isn't central to anything. But it's peaceful, affordable and has all the other qualities that urbanites like about the country. It does not have a big demand for photographers. So Jim kept his studio in the city.

For a couple of years, Jim and Sandra drove back and forth every day to open the studio and wait for the telephone to ring. When a call did come in, it could be a photo assignment in the city or just about anywhere else. In the end, the downtown studio became little more than a place to answer the telephone and a departure point to wherever the assignment happened to be.

It cost a thousand a month to rent the place. And the landlord, who operated an ice plant in the back of the building, didn't notice (or care) when the furnace ran out of fuel in winter. Jim and Sandra drove 70 miles on many winter mornings, only to sit by the phone in parkas and wait for a call.

They decided, finally, that they might be better off waiting for the phone to ring in Middleville, which was warmer, a thousand a month cheaper, easier to get to in the morning and just as close to most of the assignments that came. They gave up the downtown studio and saw no drop at all in the number of calls and assignments coming in.

Dave's career transition wasn't planned. He was a middle-distance commuter, driving five days a week from his country home to a city job as a research technician. The drive didn't bother him unduly. He fitted the comfortable old Saab with a fridge and all the extras that an incurable tinkerer could devise. What bothered Dave was the job.

"I can't stand incompetence," he says.

"What he means," says his wife Maggie, "is that he's never had a boss he thinks is any smarter than he is."

Budget cuts at the research facility put Dave on a layoff list. But his talents kept him working, doing the same old job at the same old place. The only difference was that Dave was now working on "freelance" contracts rather than on salary. A little more money, a little less security. Job security wasn't a problem. Dave had just learned from his layoff that security isn't guaranteed by being on staff; and he had learned from the demand for his freelance talents that what security he did enjoy came through his skills and not his employer.

What mattered to Dave were the choices that hadn't been considered choices before. Now, for the first time, Dave was faced with choosing between continuing the daily commute to the old job, expanding his new freelance status to other contracts or trying something completely different. In the end, it came down to the country house.

"I simply decided that I want to live in the country," he says. "And I want to be mortgage-free."

For many, those two notions go together. But Dave now had some extra impetus. "Without a mortgage," he says, "I won't ever have to worry about layoffs and contracts again. That's all the security I need." Secure, and with career now a choice instead of a given, Dave decided to go to work on his own ideas. He's developing a new kind of patented motorcycle, steering kits and other doodads to keep him happily tinkering away in his big workshop in the country.

Those whose careers are easily portable don't have to worry about the big transition. But if a move to the country means a new career, a new employer or just new working hours and arrangements, then there will be a period of uncertainty.

Will the changes be as satisfying as the old working ways? Will there be too little security? Too little money? Can I go back if I don't like it?

The can-I-go-back question takes the worry out of all the others. Most careers get stale enough that a little change of pace is welcome – as long as the possibility of going back to the tried and true remains.

The clearest solution, if you qualify, is a long-term leave of absence. Academics enjoy regular, year-long sabbaticals. Many public servants can take lengthy, unpaid leaves. Even private corporations have been known to allow long leaves for valued employees. If it doesn't exist in the personnel policy, it might still be negotiable if you're eager to leave and the company wants you back. Ask. The usual arrangement is no pay but a guaranteed return to the old job under the old salary and conditions. During the time away, retirement funds and other benefits remain in place but often at the employee's expense.

Our own move to the country was arranged that way. With few resources and two preschoolers, we didn't want to cast away all security. Selling the house, the car and the furniture seemed drastic enough without also leaving a well-paid job forever. For a year, we slept better knowing that we could always change our minds. We knew, with every bluebird, wild strawberry and northern-lights night, that we would never go back. We knew it when we drove past the old place in the city – the one we had bought because it had a big shade maple and lots of yard for the kids – and saw that it had somehow shrunk into a cramped, noisy, crowded little place whose sky was a broken geometry of blue between the eaves. We wouldn't go back. But we kept the leave-of-absence safety net in place for the full 12 months for the same reason that kids leave the training wheels on the bike – just in case.

HOME TRANSITIONS

Telephones, personal computers and the dawn of the industrial diaspora have rendered most careers more mobile than they've ever been before. The house, however, is not the least little bit mobile. I know, I know. Some houses do have wheels or seams down the middle, and they arrive in the night behind a big truck. Doesn't matter. If the fairies could somehow levitate a $300,000 house in Toronto and whisk it through the sky, like one of those "wide-load" unzipped wonders, then plunk the thing down in my backyard, it would no longer be worth 300 grand – regardless of how careful the fairies were not to scratch the paint or jiggle the china. The soaring-value part of the house is firmly rooted to the sod.

This is the other side of the equity trap that makes urbanites paper-rich while feeling poor. The price of the city house keeps right on inflating, whether you stay or not. If you sell this year, you miss a fat profit next year. In real life, of course, it's always the year before next. And sooner or later, you have to choose to cash in or to live inside your paper profits forever. When a house fetches the kind of price so common today, moving isn't a quick decision. Even pausing to think about it for a month can net the cautious a couple of thousand extra.

The risk is that a move to the country, no matter how well considered, may be irreversible. You might not be able to afford to buy back into the urban housing market once it has soared off without you for a while. Thirteen years ago, we sold in a city neighbourhood where prices have quadrupled since. Our gross receipts from the sale would just about make the down payment now.

Personally, I wouldn't want to live there again, but if we had changed our minds, what then?

There are a couple of basic strategies for keeping a toehold in the urban real estate market, just in case you change your mind later. Neither one is easy, but both work.

The obvious course is to keep the city house and rent it to tenants. In the simplest scenario, you move to the country, leave the city mortgage intact and set the rent high enough to cover the city mortgage payments and expenses.

It gets complicated if you don't have enough cash to leave your city investment intact and, at the same time, buy a place in the country. You might have to rent in the country or extract some of that city equity without giving up the house.

Indeed, renting in the country is not a bad idea, regardless of the cash situation. It's an excellent idea if you don't know the area well and want a little more time to find out more about the new community. Renting makes it easier to try several places on for size, social climate, work opportunities, schools and potential hidden problems. If it doesn't work in the first community, try another. Or give it up, and move back to the old house in the city, with no investment lost other than the cost of cleaning up the mess your own tenants left.

There are several ways to extract enough equity from the city house to pay for a move to the country. The obvious route is to renegotiate the mortgage, putting a larger lien on the property and taking out the cash. The limits to such a renegotiation depend on how much the value of the house has increased since you first signed the mortgage. And it's not without a few catches: there will be service charges on a renegotiation; American homeowners could get hit with income tax on the "profits"; and mortgage payments will be higher to cover the larger loan.

When interest rates are falling, lenders are understandably reluctant to change the old mortgage to a new one with a lower rate, even though they are increasing the size of the loan. When interest rates are rising, they'll be delighted to renegotiate. Indeed, if interest rates have risen far above what you're paying on the existing mortgage, don't renegotiate a thing. Leave the cheap mortgage intact, and take out a second mortgage. You'll pay a higher rate on the second, but the rate applies only to that marginal amount borrowed. If you take a larger first, you'll pay a higher rate on the whole amount.

If you don't want to mess with the mortgages at all, there are other kinds of loans you can take against the equity in the house. Few, however, are as cheap as a mortgage. So-called "home-equity" loans and "home-improvement" loans may be less fuss than another mortgage, but do check the rates against mortgage rates. Check, especially, those clauses that allow the lender to vary the rate.

In the United States, where mortgage interest payments on a principal residence are tax deductions, it's usually better to have lots of mortgage and no other loans. But if you rent the city house to someone else, it may no longer be classified as your "principal residence." You can still deduct interest from rental income, but tax and capital-gains provisions change, and you may find yourself paying more. Yes, it's tricky.

That's the bad news. The good news is that no matter how much equity you extract, at whatever interest cost and tax complication, your city house continues to inflate in value at the same rate as every other house on the block. In Toronto, that was an increase of $26,000 for a detached bungalow from April 1987 to April 1988. If the tenants can cover the mortgage and if you don't have to sell to buy elsewhere, $26,000 is a healthy return for the headaches of keeping that toehold in the market.

The biggest headache is being an absentee landlord.

Late rent cheques, minor maintenance that becomes major if neglected, finding new tenants and just plain checking on things add up to a lot of time. And it's a lot more time if you're many miles away in the country. Property-management firms will take the work off your hands for a fee, but it's a worry and an expense no matter how you do it. And if your tenants abuse the property or lower the tone of the neighbourhood, your nice inflationary edge may have eroded by the time you return and attempt to make amends. Being an absentee landlord is worry enough, but when it's the family home and nest egg in question, the thought of what other people might be doing to it is a real middle-of-the-night lump in the bed.

The second strategy for staying in the market is a little more businesslike than risking the family home. The idea is to sell the family home and invest the equity in something of comparable value that is meant to be rented. As in any real estate deal, success comes with picking the right neighbourhood, the one that's inflating faster than the rest. Remember that the maintenance or property-management fees will cost no less than renting out the family home. But the late-night thoughts of what "they" might be doing to your old home sweet home are gone. Now it's only an investment and not a piece of family history. If the fresh country air begins to pall, you should be able to sell the rental property with sufficient capital gains to reenter the housing market at about the level you left.

In any other business, that toehold is called a "hedge." It amounts to covering bets on both sides of the fence. When you recognize it as that — as a bet — it doesn't matter where you put your equity as long as it can be counted on to follow city real estate prices as they rise. Frank and Sue moved from Ottawa to the hills of Quebec. Problems with the children and booming urban prices scared them. They worried about the financial consequences if country life didn't pan out. Ignoring Ottawa, they bought an ordinary family house in Vancouver, rented it out and counted on the Vancouver boom to be at least as good as Ottawa's. Several years later, the family crunch did come, and they decided to leave the country and go back to Ottawa. They sold the Vancouver house and used the proceeds to buy what they wanted in the Ottawa market, with no penalty for being away all those years.

No transition strategy works quite as well as doing nothing. Staying where you are generates no new costs and allows you to keep counting all those paper profits from inflation. Your children will cash in the family cow some day and thank you for it as they take the cash to a place where prices haven't soared so high.

On the other hand, it is also true that no transition strategy works quite as well as living in the country long enough to realize that you never want to go back, even if you could afford to.

KEEPING THE LINKS

▼▼▼▼▼

The trouble with dreams is that they go to such extremes. One bad day in the city, and I start to imagine a tropical island or a mountaintop in Labrador. Someplace so remote that a traffic jam is a line of ants in the strawberry preserve. The Gauguin solution.

Then I try to figure out how to jerry-rig a South Seas island shower or generate enough power to catch the evening news, and in minutes, my mental Shangri-La is a tangle of pipes and doodads that would restore the comforts of home. Maybe not that far from civilization as we know it, I say to myself. But how far? Life gets simpler and cheaper as we move farther out, but at some point short of Labrador, it begins to get more difficult again and more expensive. What are the limits of utility? And what are the limits of affordable housing? Is there someplace between downtown Toronto and Labrador where we can afford lots of space *and* Mozart and showers?

Every city and every person's idea of what civilization means will differ. So let's just identify two extreme cases and then plot a graph between them, a map of costs and services, how far they reach and what it takes to replace them.

At the upper end of the scale, Mike and his wife are building in Toronto. Not right downtown but close enough that the lot alone cost them $265,000. With interest rates at about 10 percent, let's call that $26,500 a year. Naturally, at that price, they will have every urban service that the 20th century can provide.

At the other extreme, Bud and Ruth have left the city completely behind. They're older than Mike but not old enough to retire. Bud is self-employed and Ruth's a legal secretary, so they can live just about anywhere within a reasonable drive of the nearest lawyer. Bud and Ruth paid $5,000 for a 10-acre patch of woods, then put up a cozy log cabin for another $2,000. Let's forget the house, though. They could just as easily have built a mansion. The important difference between Bud's case and Mike's is the cost of the land and the access to services. There were no services on Bud and Ruth's land. They decided to do without. The water supply is a year-round spring with a gravity-fed pipe to the house. They have batteries for the radio and small appliances. They light with kerosene lamps and manage without the rest.

Assuming that most would prefer to live somewhere between those two extremes, let's just mark them at the edges of our map of costs and services. Nearly everything in between – the access to it and the cost of it – is somehow related to the distance from the city centre.

Even the cost of the house itself is related to where it's built . . . a little bit. Construction wages are admittedly higher in big cities like Toronto, and the cost of the materials varies. But that variation is not enough to move the lines very much. We'll assume that the cost of the house is a constant and say that the significant price difference between two identical buildings is a function of where they happen to sit.

LAND-PRICE CURVE

The graph below, Figure 1, represents the way land prices fall as you move farther and farther from a city centre. The dot at the upper end of the curve is Mike, and the dot at the lower end is Bud and Ruth. The vertical axis shows the price of the land as an annual cost. Mike's annual cost was, we said, $26,500. Bud and Ruth's land cost is $500 a year. They pay no mortgage, but they do forgo the $500 a year they could earn by investing the $5,000 elsewhere.

The horizontal axis represents the distance from the city centre. The absolute numbers won't mean very much, because every city is different and because every city is lopsided.

For example, if you believe that the Eaton Centre is the middle of Toronto, you can move two miles north into ultraexpensive Rosedale or two miles south to "free" land on the bottom of Lake Ontario. Land prices don't fall away from the centre in neat, concentric circles. So

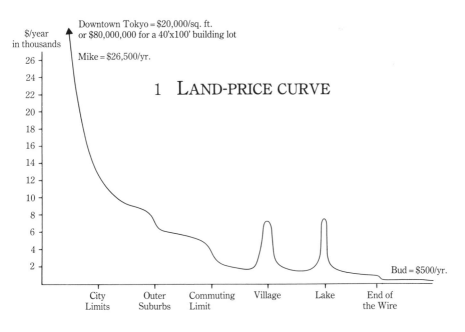

95

instead of marking the distance axis with numbers, let's mark it with more natural limits.

We'll define the "outer suburbs" as the last stop for subways and city buses and the limit of water and sewer lines. At that point, the price of land drops quite sharply. For Toronto, this might be someplace in Markham to the north and precisely at the lakeshore going south.

The "commuting limit" is the comfortable range for an average driver. For downtown Toronto, that might mean Richmond Hill. For someone who works in Manhattan, the limit might be Rhode Island. What matters is that each city has a rough fringe at the commuter limit where land prices take another drop. It's not a neatly defined line, because some drivers have the fortitude to live and drive even farther out than others. And some New York commuters would give it up long before they got to Rhode Island. More importantly, the migration of industry to the urban fringe and beyond means that fewer workers commute to the centres of cities. The cities themselves are becoming more diffuse.

Beyond the commuter limit is a band of much cheaper, rural land. It might be agricultural land or vacant land. It might be scattered lots or residential developments for those who work in the fringe industries. It might be smaller residential satellites of outlying towns and villages. What it certainly is is unserviced land too far from the city for daily commuting.

As you begin to approach those outlying towns and villages, land prices rise again. How much they rise depends on how desirable the village is. Pretty places fetch higher prices. Waterfront, historic architecture or ritzy neighbourhood status can bump up village prices to near city levels. The practical factors are water and sewers. In the United States, about half of all rural communities have public water systems, and only a third treat sewage. Public plumbing boosts the price of village lots.

At some point, not far beyond the village, prices drop to rural levels again and continue to fall gradually as you get farther and farther from public plumbing, schools and convenience stores. The price curve might have some specific little humps and vales – up for rich farmland, down for rocks and swampy ground – but the general trend is a gradual falling away as the lots move farther out.

Rural land by the water or with a spectacular view is a special case. Lakes and villages have almost the same effect on land prices: a sharp jump, with little transition between the expensive lots and the cheap ones. A private waterfront lot is costly, but a quarter of a mile back from the shore, the proximity to water is irrelevant. Close doesn't count. Similarly, a village lot that is just past the end of the public plumbing might as well be a country lot – the price drops sharply to country levels. Unlike lakeside lots, the village does have a narrow transition zone where you pay a little premium over country prices for being close to schools and shops. So although both lake and village look like spikes on the land-price curve, the village spike looks a little fatter because of that transition zone.

We cross the final price frontier about a thousand feet past the end of the last electric wire. Power and phone companies will attach new homes near the end of the line, and they don't mind filling in the gaps along the way. But the pioneer who builds far beyond the last utility pole has a hard choice to make: do without, generate your own, or pay to extend the line. The extension is more than the cost of the wire. Poles, transformer and installation come to serious dollars, even within sight of better-connected neighbours. That's why rural development creeps out in cautious little clusters. The houses follow the power lines, and the power lines follow the houses. Neither wants to be first.

The effect on the price of land is obvious – a sharp drop at the end of the line. On our graph, the drop doesn't look very dramatic because it's dwarfed by the much larger drop from the city to the country. But it is sudden. We can move two miles out of the village and compensate by driving more and walking less. We cannot move two miles past the end of the power grid and compensate by burning the lights an hour less each day. Here, the transition zone is only as wide as the bank accounts of those who are willing to extend the wired frontier.

Rural development follows the roads for the same reason it follows the utility lines: few individuals can afford to build a decent private road to an isolated lot. And few governments would be willing to build a public road to serve a single voter.

The roads and the wires form long fingers of development, reaching out into the countryside. Along these corridors, land prices fall slowly and predictably as you move away from the centres of population. Between the "fingers" are some pockets of cheaper, unserviced, less accessible land. Here, and beyond the ends of the wires, are the lowest prices. Bargains? Maybe. But only if the savings are big enough to cover the cost of making connections.

The numbers on the graph, the slopes of the curve and the relative size of the peaks and valleys vary from place to place. But the overall shape of the land-price curve will be familiar to every real estate agent and home buyer. What surprises many is the growing disproportion between the city and country ends of the curve. The line has tilted so sharply in recent years that the advantage of moving to the right is very much greater than it was.

The other surprise is that land prices have grown so quickly that the relative importance of other costs has shrunk. The new imbalance undermines the old myths about where living makes most financial sense. Staying in the city for cheaper transportation and services might have made sense once. No longer.

SERVICE COSTS

In order to see land costs in perspective, let's plot three "offsetting" costs on the same distance-from-the-city graph that we applied to land. These three (transportation, electricity and plumbing) are traditionally considered to be factors that make living in the country more expensive.

It is true that those costs go up as the distance from the city increases. And if they were true mirror images of the land-price curve, rising to fully offset falling land costs, then the old myths would hold. The shapes of these cost curves are, however, very much flatter and very much lower than the land-price curve.

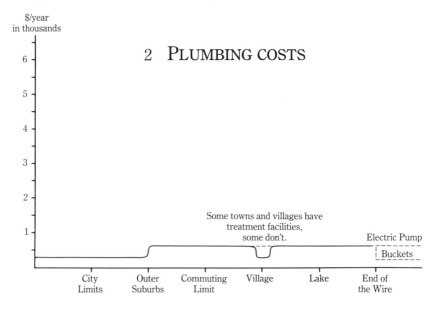

Look at the cheapest of these elements – plumbing (Figure 2). From downtown to the outer edge of the suburbs, water and sewer costs are a flat line, unrelated to distance. You pay the same no matter where you live within the city. The size of the bill depends on how much water you use and what the local rates are.

Some smaller municipalities don't meter usage. Instead, they include the cost of the service in municipal taxes. In that case, the cost to the individual is a function of distance from the centre, but moving in the opposite direction: those who live in the more expensive centre pay more taxes and thus pay more for water. That's the exception, though. The more common case is metered water at one flat rate from the city centre to the end of the pipe. Let's assume that your shower habits work out to about $250 a year.

Past the end of the pipe, plumbing costs take a step up. Out here, the householder has to provide for himself. The usual arrangement is a drilled well and a septic tank. Let's say it costs $3,000 to install the septic tank and tile bed and another $3,000 to drill the well and install a pump. That's a $6,000 initial expense, or the equivalent of $600 a year if interest rates are 10 percent. On top of that, we'll assume it costs another $50 for the extra power to run the pump. That's a total of $650 a year for the rural plumbing system. We don't need to consider the cost of fixtures and pipe; that's the same in the city or the country.

That $650 is only a guess, of course. It would certainly be more if the water table were deep in the rock or if topsoil had to be trucked in to cover the septic tank. No matter. Call it $450 or $850 or whatever, it still won't offset the land-price curve enough to be noticed.

What matters is that the cost of the rural system doesn't change anymore as the distance from the city increases. Land costs keep dropping, but the plumbing costs quit rising. The graph takes a sharp step up at the end of the city pipe, then resumes its flat shape until you reach the end of the power line, somewhere between here and the sunset. At that point, you can no longer run the pump and so must make do with buckets of water for drinking and bathing and a privy instead of a flush. Your plumbing costs drop to the price of an occasional replacement bucket.

Moving to a small town with public plumbing will lower the cost to near city levels. But, in general, the cost is constant in the country, whether you live one block beyond the last city pipe or 500 miles to the north.

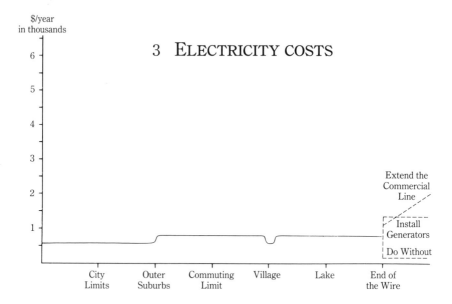

$/year
in thousands

3 ELECTRICITY COSTS

6 —

5 —

4 —

3 —

2 —

1 —

Extend the
Commercial
Line

Install
Generators

Do Without

City   Outer   Commuting   Village   Lake   End of
Limits   Suburbs   Limit   the Wire

Electricity costs display a similar geography (Figure 3), perhaps with smaller steps at the city limits. In rural areas, many power companies raise the price per kilowatt-hour, charging country customers a little more to compensate for higher maintenance costs. Again, there may be a dip in the rate for an outlying village, where a local utility company can negotiate something close to the city rate. Power costs, like plumbing costs, remain constant as you move farther and farther into the country. The graph remains flat.

The big jump (or drop) happens when you move off the existing power grid. Beyond this point, you have to choose whether to do without, install generators or pay the power company to extend the line.

If you do without, like Bud and Ruth, power costs drop to near nothing. Batteries for the radio, kerosene for the lamps, a few more candles than the rest of us use.

If you opt for home-generated power, costs could take a big step up. Even if wind or waterfall will turn the generator for nothing, the high initial outlay for the equipment has to be considered. If you invest $10,000 at the start, that's the equivalent of $1,000 a year. Then batteries and maintenance add recurrent costs.

Similarly, building power lines to the nearest point on the utility's grid involves a capital outlay, then ongoing energy charges. In this case, however, the initial outlay is distance-dependent. That is, the farther you are from the end of the line, the higher will be the initial

100

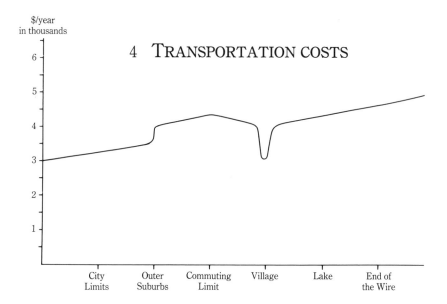

$/year
in thousands

6

5

4

3

2

1

4 TRANSPORTATION COSTS

| City Limits | Outer Suburbs | Commuting Limit | Village | Lake | End of the Wire |

cost to extend it. So connecting to the commercial grid is not a step up to another flat line but a new and steeper slope that raises the cost higher as you move farther out.

In or out of the city, transportation is a major cost (Figure 4). Amortizing the cost of the car itself, then adding fuel, maintenance, parking and repairs means that most of us pay thousands of dollars a year for the privilege of driving. The cost is certainly distance-related, to a degree. Remember that the biggest cost, the car itself, must be paid whether we drive a block to the office or a thousand miles. Parking works the other way: the closer we live to the centre of the city, the higher are the costs of the real estate upon which the car spends most of its time. On the other hand, urbanites have greater access to subsidized public transportation. They, at least, have the option of using buses, bikes and feet for some of the family trips. So the transportation curve starts high on the $ axis to cover the basic costs of the car, then climbs slowly as greater distances demand more fuel, maintenance, and so on.

At the outer suburbs, where the buses stop, the transportation curve takes a step up. No more sending the kids to hockey practice on the bus – you have to drive them in. Costs continue to rise as a function of distance and family size until you get near an outlying village. Then you begin to substitute, shopping for staples in the nearer village rather than driving into the city, transferring bank accounts, doc-

101

tor and dentist. Costs drop as you move closer to the village, then take an even sharper dip for those who live within the village or close enough to walk. Within this range, feet take over again.

When we total all those distance costs, the sum very closely resembles the transportation curve, since transport is the largest element (Figure 5). The overall effect is a gently rising curve with a short, sharp jump at the outer limits of buses and sewers, a gentle drop within driving distance of village services and a sharp drop within walking distance of the village. Beyond the end of the power grid, the cost curves can strike off in a variety of directions as individuals choose different ways of coping.

Beyond the end of the power lines, all we can say for sure is that life gets harder, more complicated or more expensive. If the only reason for moving beyond the power grid is the marginally cheaper land that lies there, look again at the land-price curve. How much are you likely to save by taking that last step into the woods? And how much is it likely to cost you in convenience, money and work? If your reason for looking to the farther reaches is a desire for more isolation, that's fine. But strictly on the economics of it, the mountaintop in Labrador is not necessarily the cheapest choice.

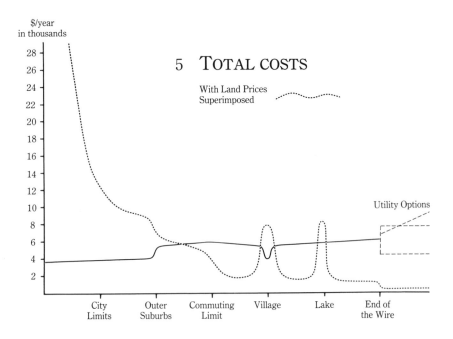

The final graph (Figure 6) combines the distance-related costs with the land-price curve. The resulting "total" isn't a real total. It doesn't include groceries, library fines and a zillion other things. But it does highlight the costs that change as you live closer to or farther from the city. In the city and suburbs, land is a major component of the cost of living. Costs fall as you move farther out, despite the relatively minor increases in rural transportation and service costs. Those increases are not significant until you move past the end of the roads and wires.

Other "wire" services (cable TV, telephone and fax) might be available wherever the electric grid runs. There are exceptions. Commercial cable companies prefer to serve dense concentrations of subscribers. So you can get cable hookups in some villages but rarely in the open countryside. Private-line phone service is not available everywhere in the country, even where the poles exist. You can substitute. You can get a satellite dish instead of cable or catch your favourites on the local channels that an antenna brings in. You can write letters instead of phoning and faxing or learn to live with the party line. What you cannot do is convince commercial services to extend the grid just for you.

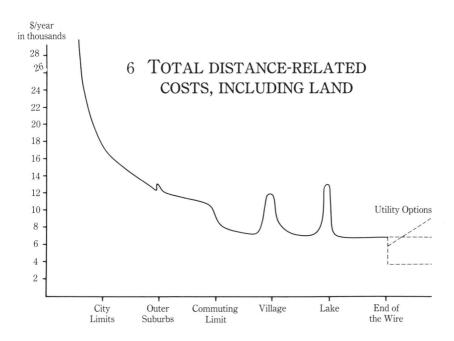

103

Land and utility structures vary so much from place to place that even the most accurate statistical averages won't mean very much. If you're plotting a move, gather data particular to that region. You can get land prices from real estate agents or from the classified ads in local papers. A call to the utility company will tell you which areas they serve and which they don't and how much it will cost to extend the service. Plot the data on a map. Chances are, you'll see that the big savings come from moving beyond the city but still within the power grid. You can control transportation costs by moving closer to a village with shops and services.

QUALITY OF RURAL SERVICES

So far, we've talked about the costs of rural services and substitutes. But what about the quality? Is there a difference between city services and the country? Transportation is the big item and a big chunk of time out of both rural and urban lives (1.46 hours a day in the city, 1.29 hours a day in the country). Regrettably, public transportation barely exists outside the city. In the country, getting around is by car. You might find an intercity bus that stops in a small town or village, and perhaps a village taxi. But not as a matter of public policy. Not in North America. Europe does a much better job for its rural residents. So do India, Cuba, Luzon and most of the Third World. The best that can be said is that many North American cities are as badly served as the countryside. Perhaps that's why only 6 percent of American workers commute on public transport.

Other services normally administered by municipalities make a checkered comparison. It depends on the quality of the local government and on its tax base. Here, in a widely scattered township of several thousand, garbage is collected once a week. The neighbouring township has a dump but no collection service. Other townships ignore the problem and let the ditches fill with rubbish, which is another good reason to know the township well before you buy a property.

Similarly, road maintenance, potholes and snowploughs may be a problem in one tax district and not in the next.

Electric power is administered across wider territories, by provincial and statewide power authorities. In theory, that should mean that rural and urban service within those broad jurisdictions is the same. Yes and no. The cost, as we've seen, is affected by differential rural rates. Costs rise slightly as you leave the city and rise substantially as you pass beyond the boundaries of the existing grid.

The quality of electricity doesn't change, a city kilowatt being indistinguishable from its country cousin. But the reliability of delivery does vary. Rural power lines are more vulnerable to storm damage and lower priority for repairs. There are more power interruptions, and they last longer. They also matter less (with one important exception). They matter less because there are fewer traffic lights, elevators, underground passages and other vulnerable bottlenecks that bring life to a halt when power goes off in the city. With a wood stove, a hand pump on the spare well and plenty of candles, we can survive blackouts that would bring great cities to their knees. Our only discomfort is moving a little closer to the light to read.

The exception to the rule of rural indifference to blackouts is the home computer. The very machine that makes it practical for millions more to work outside the city is absolutely dependent on the current. When a limb falls across the wire, the computer forgets what it was doing. Fortunately, there are two solutions to the problem. One is to add off-the-shelf equipment to protect against power interruptions and variations. The second is to tell the local office of the power company (personally and in writing) that you work at home with computers and that you'll sue the pants off them if they don't notify you in advance of every planned power cut. The planned cuts (for maintenance or new house hookups) can be a bigger nuisance than storm damage. You can see a thunderstorm coming and shut down the machine, but the deliberate cuts by the power company come as a nasty surprise if you aren't on the list to be notified.

Rural telephone service, like rural power, is subject to occasional interruptions. Unlike the kilowatt, however, telephone quality is far from uniform. The private-line service that is the norm in cities is simply unavailable in some country districts. In other locales, you can hook onto a multiparty line at a standard fee but have to pay ruinous penalties for a private line. The party line used to be a social occasion or an invasion of privacy, depending on how you felt about those things. Now it's something more. Now it completely precludes the use of new touch-tone services, computer modems, direct dialling or anything else that assumes a dedicated line. We can hope that government regulators will eventually wake up to the fact that rural businesses and individuals need the new technology of the wired world even more than the urbanites do. In the meantime, ask the local telephone company what level of service is available before you move your modem to the country.

PUTTING IT IN PERSPECTIVE

Lest you look at the list of rural disadvantages and conclude that perhaps life is simpler in the city after all, consider the survey that asked some new rural residents of western Canada about the disadvantages of their country locales. Water supply and quality were mentioned by 10 percent, while 8 percent complained about garbage disposal and 4 percent named sewage problems. Nobody mentioned blackouts, poor phone service or the lack of public transportation. Fewer than 4 percent felt isolated. And 95 percent said they were satisfied with their lives in the country, despite any problems they could name.

FAMILY LIFE

▼▼▼▼▼

Moving to the country presents a classic dilemma in parent-child warfare. Deep down in your heart of hearts, you're certain it's the best thing for them, they'll thank you for it at nostalgia time, it's just what you would have loved as a child. Clean, safe, healthy, wholesome. And the kids, of course, will say they hate it. "Why do we have to live in the boonies?" they'll whine in the spinach voice. "It's so BOOOOORRING!"

Worse than that, you will wonder yourself if what you're doing is really the best thing for them. Don't.

First of all, there's a five-year period in nearly every child's life when the world is supposed to be boring. It's in the rules. It's especially supposed to be boring if adults find it fascinating. Secondly, it's better that they should be bored where it's a 10-mile walk to the nearest shopping mall. By the time they get there, they'll be too tired to get into trouble.

So don't ask the kids where they want to move. They'll only want to move to Disney World. And by the time they outgrow that, they're into the five-year period when they think that a crowded beach is more fun than an empty one, that any noise is better than quiet and that a good night's sleep should begin at dawn.

Still, those of us foolhardy enough to have children will pause on the brink of any move and wonder how it will affect the kids. Even if we ignore their criteria (distance to the nearest Dairy Queen, number of hunks in the neighbourhood, enough pavement for skateboards), we wonder about the things that don't concern them yet: Are the schools any good? What about health and safety? Will their experiences be too narrow outside the city? What kind of life mate might they find in a place like this?

NO SAFE PLACE

Marianne, from New York City, married a doctor and moved to Lanark, a sleepy village of 480 people. It took the New Yorker and the doctor three years to find their Eden. They finally chose Lanark because it promised to be the best possible place to raise their infant son. Safe, quiet, friendly, clean – all the things that New York would never be. Two weeks after she told me that, the health department announced that half the well water in the village was unfit to drink. A double murder put a pall on things, then the husband broke his ankle on the ice.

The Waltons bought a heritage farmhouse and got the whole family involved in the restoration. Two of the daughters contracted histoplasmosis from the heritage bat dung in the attic and eaves, severely damaging their vision.

The Leblancs of New Brunswick left city dangers to live in the woods and then sickened from the aerial spraying meant to control the spruce budworm.

Duffy Sheridan went looking for the one place in the world isolated enough to guarantee peace, freedom and wilderness. He finally chose the Falkland Islands. After the Argentineans and the British finished their squabble, Duffy could hardly go out of his house because of the mines.

There is no safe place. Armstrong, British Columbia, population 2,706, is hundreds of miles and a couple of mountain ranges removed from city traffic. And yet Susan and Keith worry whenever their child Jordie, 5, goes out to play. "It's the traffic," Susan explains. "They come speeding around this corner, taking the shortcut to the highway . . ." Susan leaves the sentence unfinished as another set of tires squeals. Keith, a former rodeo bull rider, gets up to look out the door again – the third time in 15 minutes.

Is that clear, parents? The worries come with the kids, not the location. Population density has nothing to do with it. Moving merely changes some of the things we worry about. We don't worry about alley muggings and freeway shootings; we do worry about needing a doctor when the lane is plugged with snow. We don't worry about drugs in the school – we do worry about teenage friends who drink and drive. We don't worry about the wolves and the bears that live in the woods, but we have learned to train the children to keep out of the woods in hunting season.

Urban or rural, the real dangers are the ones we haven't prepared the children for, the ones that happen in other places. City kids know that the man in the open raincoat hasn't really lost his clothes, and they know not to leave their money on the park bench while they play. They're prepared for that. They worry, instead, about snakes and spiders and the thing in the woods. Rural parents, on the other hand, have confidence that their children know enough to avoid poison ivy and snakes. They worry, instead, that the children won't understand about the man in the raincoat or about leaving their money on a park bench.

There are summer camps that prepare city kids for rural survival:

starting fires, following a creek downstream and all that stuff. There is, alas, no counterpart for rural kids where they can learn urban survival skills, like reading bus maps and distinguishing the hustlers from the friendly strangers.

In the absence of an urban camp, we have to teach them ourselves or make the ultimate decision for them: "Well, kids, we've figured all the angles, and there really are more advantages to living in the country than in the city. So it doesn't matter if you're not prepared for urban survival, you're better off out here."

No. It wouldn't wash. Our children will have to cope with the city, even if it's only to visit or to study or to take advantage of a job transfer. It's up to us to manage country living in such a way that they won't be unprepared.

NEIGHBOURS

It's not that children have less stimulating contacts in rural society – they have fewer contacts. And the more isolated you want to be, the fewer contacts your children will have or the farther you'll have to drive them to keep the contacts alive. There. I've said it. That's the worst of it. That and the ugly truth that children are, at times, less concerned about the quality of their social lives than about the quantity.

When Beth was 6, she spent a fortnight with a city aunt and uncle. They took her swimming, on picnics and shopping expeditions – all the normal kid-on-a-summer-visit activities. She wasn't particularly impressed with the malls or the pool or the park. They were too familiar to interest even a country girl. Her favourite time seemed to be the early evenings, when the adults were busy with meals and newspapers and the neighbourhood children roamed the sidewalks in shrieking little packs, playing games and moving from house to house to avoid bedtime and parental attention.

She was an especially quiet child, however, and the depth of this interest, or any other, could only be guessed. When it was time to leave, the uncle took Beth aside and asked her if she had had a good time. She nodded.

"Well, tell me what you liked about it, then. Was it the swimming pool? The day we went to the park? What did you like best?"

"Neighbours," she said and dashed away for one last round with the sidewalk gang.

Now, at 16, Beth still cycles more than three miles to swim at a crowded public beach. There are weeds in the water, rocks and cigarette butts in the sand and, on hot days, little room to spread a towel. She has the choice of travelling a tiny fraction of that distance to a private beach where the water is cleaner and the crowd nonexistent, but Beth still prefers a crowd to the peace and quiet. Neighbours.

They aren't all like that. Beth's brother plays happily by himself and considers swimming to be something one does with water; and clean, close water is better than distant, dirty water. Who knows why they're different? Not me. But I do know that if you move children to the country, some of them are going to want neighbours. The neighbours don't have to be close enough to hear you shave, but if they're too far beyond the walking limits of a 6-year-old, beware. The 6-year-old will drive you crazy if you don't drive her to the neighbours often enough.

Some of the old back-to-the-landers went with the theory that rural isolation would pull the family closer together. Children would play with their brothers and sisters, spend more time with their parents and form strong bonds, bonds that urban pressures had stretched or broken. Balderdash. Almost. It does work to a point. Given enough time together, brothers and sisters will eventually figure out for themselves that it's more fun to get along with one another than to fight. But then, lots of urban siblings figure that out too.

It's nice when siblings learn to play together. But it's necessary that they learn to play with neighbours, even strangers, too. Thoreau didn't take kids to Walden with him. It wouldn't have been the same if he had.

Family life never stays the same for long. It evolves. In the primordial stage of parenthood, we wondered whether those little bundles of ammonia and milk would ever learn to walk. And as soon as they did, we wished they hadn't. Will they ever talk? And then they won't stop. They chatter until we're ready to plug our ears with wax, and then they quit talking altogether, retiring behind closed doors to throw a baseball at the ceiling for seven solid months. At every stage, it is certain that the parents will be one stage behind. Life will end if she doesn't have a pony; but by the time you surrender to the pleas, find the pony, build the shed, fence the field, buy the saddle and sign up for three years of riding lessons, she has taken up hair drying and has decided riding is dumb. Ponies live at least 17 years longer than any adolescent's interest in them. Whether you move to the country, move

111

to the city or stay where you are, it will only suit the children for a little while. Then it will be dumb – no matter what it is. So do whatever it is you want to do for you.

Just be aware that as the children evolve, so do their social interests. We can't plan a whole family life style around those fleeting interests, but we can anticipate some of the childhood needs and accommodate them most of the time.

This will be redundant to anyone who has already survived child rearing. If that's you, skip ahead. You've earned a break. This is for the new owners of the milk-and-ammonia bundles, for parents who have visions of the precious things skipping through wildflower meadows forever. The important thing is not to plan a long-term move around the short-term skipping-through-the-flowers stage. It helps to imagine that the baby will become several different people in succession: a preschooler, a student, a pubescent hormone bomb and a reasonably independent teen.

PRESCHOOL

The preschoolers appear to be most content with an isolated rural life, especially if they have one or two parents at home all day. They really do loll in meadows and marvel at natural mysteries. This is the time when all you seemingly need to provide is a swing, some miniature replicas of whatever tools the adults use, lots of time to answer questions, and pets. Seemingly. Then you take these super-intelligent loving wonders to town, and they respond to other people by sticking thumb in mouth and hanging onto your leg. Aha! They need to interact with other children. In the absence of neighbours, you'll have to provide. Here's what we found:

First, every village and town within shopping distance offers some kind of lessons for kids – dancing, swimming, gymnastics, music, diaper hockey or backgammon. It doesn't matter what it is, as long as there are other kids doing it. If the village is large enough to have a recreation committee, they will know what's going on. Otherwise, watch the local paper or the notices on the grocery-store bulletin board. Sometimes, a church will sponsor preschool activities. Alternatively, service clubs or even parents can get things organized.

Whenever possible, arrange the child's timetable to coincide with yours. If that means evening gymnastics rather than afternoon swimming, so be it. For several years, our weekly shopping trips were planned to coincide with a play group – 20 or so rural families who took over a church basement once a week to let the little ones romp together. The timing meant there was no extra driving, and everybody was happy.

The play group eventually evolved into something even better – a well-organized toy-lending library. The parents formed a cooperative, got a small starting grant, bought a stock of high-quality toys, took permanent space above the town library and opened once a week for playtime on the floor. Whatever catches junior's fancy can be taken home for a week and returned. The kids get a regular change of toys and a visit once a week with what amounts to neighbours.

Larger places have more regular preschool programmes. We found a Montessori school in a town of 5,000. Montessori took the children from the age of 2½ and were happy to have them two mornings a week, which was just the right substitute for highest-quality neighbourhood play. In a pinch, we have enrolled in part-time day care. Not for the usual reasons, but just to give some country kids a place to meet their peers.

It is never quite so easy as an old-fashioned neighbourhood, where they disappeared after breakfast and came home for lunch with three friends in tow. But then, that is a disappearing ideal in the best urban neighbourhoods. Even there, with fewer parents at home all day and more worries abroad, there aren't many places left where it is still advisable to turn the kids loose on the neighbourhood.

One way or another, it may be necessary to engineer some social contacts for the preschoolers and then drive them there. The alternative is not a perpetually happy babe in the wildflower meadow. The alternative is a thumb-sucking pant-leg puller when strangers drive up the lane.

EARLY SCHOOL

For a few happy years, the parental transit system gets to take a break. The big yellow bus does most of the driving, and school soaks up much of the excess energy and much of the need that youngsters have for one another. It's not a neglect of parental duty; they are getting a fuller social life than they were when you had to organize it.

The school, for a while, becomes the neighbourhood. It is play and friends and interaction with a whole new set of adults. It can provide sports, fun and social events. And in general, the more isolated the

113

community, the stronger the role of the school. It is much more than a school in the urban sense. It becomes a community centre.

Let's set aside the question of academic quality for a moment and consider first the rural school's value as a substitute for neighbours. Can it provide a social and emotional environment as constructive as the city alternatives?

It can, but it's not a function of the size of the school or its budget. The social quality is more often a matter of parental involvement. Think of it this way: education policies are set by boards and government agencies led by people who live in cities. They have a narrow notion that school is for learning and that mixing with peers is something students do in the neighbourhood after school. The idea that school can be the centre of a community is not a big-city idea. So the local principal and the teacher, even in a rural school, may have limited scope to encourage the kinds of activities that teach youngsters how to get along with one another, how to cooperate and how to be well-rounded, responsible persons. The principal and staff are directed to teach the set curriculum. That's all. The rest – all the good things that happen in some rural schools – happens when parents get involved and help the staff do what they never have enough time or money to do alone.

It is more than the addition of free labour to the system. It becomes a dynamic of mutual reinforcement. When parents help with the field trips, pageants, concerts, sports days, picnics and potluck suppers, both teachers and pupils are prone to pull up their socks. Bullies are less likely to bully when parents are around. Lazy teachers are less likely to slough off students with busywork. Pupils are less likely to blame bad grades on the teacher.

It isn't a matter of taking control or of pushy parents interfering where professionals should hold sway. It's a matter of involvement with the process. It's means and ends. The old way was to turn the kids over to the best system taxes could buy and expect them to emerge in 12 years' time, educated and ready for work or university. The involved way is to assume the system will have shortcomings, then to step forward and do something about it.

That's not to say that in every country school, parents can or will participate in the process. But in the smaller schools, where budgets are small and the power over distant school boards is weak, parental involvement may be the only way to make an urban system work for rural needs.

Here's how it happened in one public school, 50 miles from its board headquarters in the city of Brockville. It's a midsized school for a rural area, drawing about 200 pupils from a seven-mile radius. Changes began when the principal held an open house and sparked the organization of a parents' committee. The initial concern was second-language instruction. Parents felt that French classes should start earlier and last longer. The distant board had decided differently. Parents and some local teachers closed ranks, demanded changes and got them.

Still flushed with success, parents learned that the board, in the interest of saving money, proposed to hold the line on nonacademic expenses (music, sports and activities) by stopping the expansion of such services to growing schools (mostly rural) and allowing them only where they already existed (the urban schools). In effect, Brockville would keep its extensive music, drama and art programmes, and the country schools would not get the programmes, no matter how much they grew. Country parents filled an auditorium in Brockville and demanded that the board reverse the decision.

One thing led to another. Parents raised money to augment the budget for field trips and then went along to help with the supervision. Parents volunteered to supervise public skating on the school rink one night a week and then organized a ski-and-skate exchange to swap outgrown equipment. Parents helped on the playground and then raised the money to re-equip it. Parents coached pupils who needed extra help with reading or math. Parents painted scenery and played the piano for plays and concerts. The activity took on social dimensions with a winter carnival, spring fling, parent-and-child sports, potluck suppers and a community picnic. It spread to include many seniors whose children had long since left the school. Not every parent was involved, not even a majority. But even that limited involvement was enough to ease the school far beyond the three Rs, which the staff was paid to teach and to which they could have retreated. The school became a neighbourhood. It gave isolated youngsters a social life and perhaps a hint of what social responsibility can mean.

One mother, herself schooled in a large city, saw the difference in the attitudes of the students. "I walked into the school just as the bell rang for recess," she recalls. "The younger ones were squirming on the floor of the corridor, struggling with snowsuits and boots. I thought they'd be trampled when the grade sixes burst out, but instead, the bigger ones stopped to help. Nobody told them to. They just got down on the floor and pulled on boots until all the little kids were dressed."

After grade six, the country students travel to a senior school in a nearby town of 9,000. I asked one shy country girl how they were treated. There are a lot more of the town kids, I said. Do they make fun of the country kids or act snobby?

She looked surprised that I would even think such a silly question. The senior school has its share of social divisions and adolescent cruelties, but none of that happens along geographic lines. Not anymore. The days when the town sophisticates could dismiss the visiting country kids as bumpkins are gone. They watch the same television programmes, share the same heroes and slang, dress alike and study the same curriculum to the same state or provincial standard. The biggest difference seems to be that the smaller schools have less equipment and more of a family feeling.

The lesson is: If you're moving with children to the country, get involved with the school. Meet the principal. Join the home and school committee or the PTA. Bake cookies, chaperone, volunteer. Those things, in a rural school, are at least as important as the ABCs.

QUALITY OF EDUCATION

The public school systems of North America are increasingly under attack. In the United States, scores on the Scholastic Aptitude Tests, widely used for university entrance, have been dropping steadily since 1965. In Canada, universities have added remedial reading and writing for first-year students. Parents respond by removing children from the public system: between 1969 and 1986, Canadian public school enrolment fell by 11 percent, while private enrolment rose 27 percent. Their motives may be mixed (in the United States, race and religion play a role), but the results are dramatic. Millions of North American kids now attend private schools; and by 1982, John Naisbitt in *Megatrends* had estimated that a million more were being educated at home.

If the public school system is failing, there is no clear evidence that it fails rural students more than urban ones. The large urban schools might have more laboratories, computers and libraries than the small country schools, but the results don't divide along those lines. The best that can be said about who fails and who succeeds in the public school system is closer to home than that. Successful students appear to come from a certain kind of home. Parental levels of education, income and encouragement provide the geography of academic success.

The stereotype of disadvantaged rural students is a relic of the days when rural parents had less education and lower incomes than city parents. Now the wellsprings of academic success are distributed more evenly.

We have already seen that rural and urban incomes are converging. Similarly, educational attainment has moved beyond the city limits. In Canadian small towns (5,000 to 10,000), the percentage of persons with secondary and vocational diplomas is 14.6 percent, compared with the metropolitan value of 15.4 percent. Regional figures are even more surprising. While the rural/urban disparity persists in places like Newfoundland, British Columbia has, by some measures, tended to reverse the gap. There, 18.8 percent of rural (nonfarm) residents hold secondary and vocational diplomas, surpassing the metropolitan areas' 18.1 percent. And small-town degree holders, at 8.4 percent, have nearly reached the metropolitan level of 10.1 percent.

In the United States, the distribution of success has changed even more markedly. There, especially in the older cities of the Northeast and the industrial Midwest, city cores have decayed. Educated, white-collar families moved to the suburbs in the 1950s and farther in the 1970s. It is no longer true that privilege lives at the centre of large American cities. Government attempts to restore the cores with sports domes, convention centres and other post-religion cathedrals have done little to redress the human imbalance.

Beyond the public school system, rural parents have been no less ready than their urban counterparts to create alternatives to state education. In scores of small communities, parents have organized and run their own local schools with paid, qualified teachers. There is no guarantee that an alternative school can provide a better education than the public system. It certainly isn't any easier on the parents: managing by committee work bees and bake sales is never as easy as entrusting the job to a school board. But there is some comfort in knowing that at least it's possible to provide a decent education, even in places where the official school may be too far away, too underfunded or too neglected to be of much use.

Finally, there is always the possibility of teaching children at home.

Given the time and the resources, there is little reason a qualified parent or, better still, a group of parents, can't educate the child as well as the school can. But for an isolated rural family, it has to be a last resort. No matter how hard you try, you can't teach children how to fit into the larger world by keeping them home to yourself. They need other children and other adults. They need a neighbourhood and a school, or a school where the parents are sufficiently involved to put neighbourly feelings into the school.

The alternatives to public education are hard to organize and hard to maintain. They don't always work as well as the public system. But at least we know that education is not a simple choice between well-funded city schools and poor country ones. There are also good country schools, the prospect of making mediocre schools better and a few possibilities beyond.

ADOLESCENCE

Adolescents become aware of what rural living means in funny ways, often through the eyes of others. They assume that everybody can start at the back door and ski for miles through virgin snow, take a short walk to a clean beach, bike down tree-shaded lanes, have pets and picnics whenever they like, sit in a tree alone to dream, jump in haystacks and eat strawberries until they pop. That's the everyday, and therefore dumb. Hardly worth a whit when compared to a rare and valued experience like hanging out in a shopping mall. And then, little by little, they begin to see.

Like Kirsten and the pony. She was at that age when all she wanted was a pony. Everybody but her took riding lessons. Every family but ours went to riding stables on Sunday afternoons to rent horses. She was feeling terribly, terribly deprived.

Then one day, I drove her to school early for some forgotten reason. And there at the end of the lane, not 300 yards from the house, was a pony. A big pony. An unattached pony, wandering down the road. We slowed to get around it, Kirsten's hands and nose pressed flat to the glass.

"Dad," she began, in that wistful voice that made the rest of the words redundant. "Dad, if the pony's still there tonight when I come home from school, can I put it in the front pasture until we can find the owner?"

"If you can catch it," I agreed, certain that there were sufficient "ifs" in all of that to keep us both happy. "But we'll have to find the owners and return it."

"I know that, Dad. What do you think I am, a little kid or something? Like, 'It followed me home, can I keep it?' Jeez."

Then, like a little kid again, "Ooooohhh, I hooope it's still theeere toniiight, IhopeIhopeIhopeIhope." I'm sure her toes were crossed inside her boots. Far be it from me to burst her balloon, but in my cynical core, I knew the pony would wander away or the owner would come, long before we got home.

The owner came, desperate. Not desperate to find the pony but desperate to find someplace to keep it, where it (Melanie) wouldn't immediately jump the fence and wander off causing trouble again. Melanie, it seemed, was lonely. The owner had had the pony from her own adolescence and was now a grown woman with a city career, much too busy for riding.

"I don't suppose . . . no, that would be asking too much. . . . But then . . . maybe . . . well, would you mind if I put Melanie in your front pasture while I arrange something permanent for her? It would only be for a day or two."

My wife agreed that a couple of days wouldn't do any harm. They sealed the deal with a pot of tea and commiserations on the trials of wandering stock. In the end, they agreed that Melanie could stay for the summer, as long as she didn't need shelter or hay.

"Do you have children?" asked the delighted owner. "If you do, I could leave the saddle and bridle here too. She'd be happier if someone were riding her . . . if it's no bother."

No, it would be no bother at all.

In the meantime, I was driving Kirsten home from school. A day in school was hardly a comma in our conversation from the morning.

"Do you think it will still be there?" she said, instead of "Hello."

"What do you mean?" I lied. "Will what be there?"

"Oh, Dad!" Kids are so easily disgusted, even when their toes are crossed. "Ooohh, IhopeIhopeIhopeIhopeIhopeIhope." And, of course, it was there. In the field. With saddle and bridle. All hers until the snow next winter would cover the grass.

It was a magic world for at least a week. A world where dreams come true. And then, inevitably, it was ordinary again. Like the pets and the lake and the forest and all the other ordinary things.

When Melanie came back the following spring, something even better happened. Some city people built a cottage, barely half a mile away. Neighbours! Better still, they had a daughter just Kirsten's age. Danielle from the city and Kirsten from the country were soon thick as thieves. Naturally, each thought the other's life was ideal. Danielle, who really had had riding lessons (and a long commute to the stables), was enchanted with the idea of having a mount at the door, ready to carry you off to the lake or down the quiet, woody lanes. She came every day to ride. She brought cousins and city friends, who likewise marvelled at the notion of living in a place where a Melanie was possible, something so perfect that sort of followed one home.

Kirsten's humdrum, ordinary, boring country life was suddenly something envied. And the enviers were people she herself envied. 'Twas ever thus. The social handicaps were, for a little while, seen through other eyes.

A Melanie doesn't wander down every country lane looking for an adolescent girl to take her home. That was special. But it did teach us that no matter what kind of home we make for our children, it will never satisfy all of their needs all of the time. If it did, they might never leave, and that would probably be worse. So we might as well find a place that suits the grown-ups and most of the children's friends.

COMING OF AGE

The crunch comes with the first stirrings of romance. For the first time, the problems of growing up in the country cannot be solved with a little parental attention. When they were tots, we only had to find them friends a few times a week. When they began school, they found their own friends, and all we had to do was help make the school as much a neighbourhood as it was a place to learn. In early adolescence, they had independent social lives, limited only by the range of self-propulsion: bikes, legs and a middle-distance pony.

To that point, raising kids in the country was little different from raising kids in the city. The distances were a little longer for the family taxi. And we had to be a little more conscientious about providing that service because the alternatives were fewer. But there were few problems that time couldn't solve and lots of compensations that even the children could see in their lucid moments.

Love, or the imagining of it, changes all the rules. No boy in his right mind would ever walk my daughter home from a school dance. They wouldn't get here until breakfast, and then, of course, she'd be grounded for life. Dating, so they tell me, loses something when

120

your parents do the driving. I'll have to take their word for it.

It's different in small towns and villages. Dating there can be simpler – simpler even than for city teens. In the village, you can walk home from just about anywhere. Of course, all the neighbours will see, but at least village teens don't have to endure the horrors of the parent-chauffeured date. Don't have to. Just as the cows don't have to eat the grass on the other side of the fence.

The problem is that teens can find the boy next door as familiar and boring as family. Maybe it's a natural instinct to keep the gene pool stirred. Whatever.

When I was younger and understood these things, our big, rural school district was split in two by a range of steep hills that ate the lower gears of school buses and separated two small, scattered communities by several miles of uninhabited switchback road. There was an unwritten law that at a certain age, your face would fall off if you dated someone within walking distance. We dated the girls from the other side of the hill, and the boys over there dated the girls on our side. We passed on Saturday nights at the top of the hill and waved.

Parents be warned: Don't choose the town over the country just to ease your future teenager's love life. Nothing eases that. It will be complicated and far away no matter where you live.

All you have to remember is that at some point (about a week after you notice that you haven't had to remind them to brush their hair recently), the mealtime conversation takes regular turnings to the subject of cars and driving licences – who has one, who's getting one, how much faster are youthful reactions than those of the dangerous oldsters on the road. Little things like that. The message, in case your children are more subtle than mine, is: Being driven around by parents is dumb, boring and a humiliating reminder of childhood dependence (last week).

Here's where rural living diverges from any comparable urban experience. Sure, city kids want to drive and want to ride around with their friends, whether or not they have anywhere to go. But for city kids, the alternative is not to stay at home; the alternative is to walk or take a bus to where the action is. Rural teens have to stay at home or arrive with their parents.

It is, of course, completely unfair. Taxpayers, rural and urban, subsidize public transit in the cities, where people are close enough to walk. Yet out in the country, where everywhere is too far to walk, residents are left to fend for themselves. Most of us manage with cars and are quite content to pay that price. Those who suffer are the teens and the elderly who have reached an age when they would rather not drive or can't afford to drive.

While waiting for the politicians to do the right thing, what can a parent do? Part of the answer is teaching youngsters to drive. That's neither a whole solution nor an unflawed one. When a kid can sprain an ankle falling off a sidewalk, who would be crazy enough to trust her with the car? You can insist they take a proper driving course, make them pay for their own insurance in an effort to instil some sense of the risks involved. You can make rules about calling home, early curfews, no alcohol, and you'll still worry.

Even if you've raised a couple of Saint Teens, you'll worry when they're out with friends who aren't. They're not going to get mugged on the subway, but that doesn't guarantee their safety.

It would be misleading to leave any discussion of rural family life on such an uneasy note. Most of the time, for most rural families, life differs very little from urban lives.

We had days when our berry-brown tots raced the spring goats down the hill and all tumbled together at the bottom. There were full-moon nights when we skied home through an owl-enchanted forest, the children's eyes as wide as the moon. There were lots more family games and jokes because we were the only friends around at the time. There were popcorn Sunday afternoons around the fire, long snowy hikes to find the exactly right tree for Christmas, spring days of drinking sweet icy sap from the buckets, cool swims on hot August days and belly-flopping piles of leaves in fall. All of those days were better than we ever imagined they could be when we packed two babes to leave the city. None of those days lasted long enough or happened often enough.

And there are joys and adventures we may never know about, secret lives that children have, the things that later become nostalgia. I discovered one the other day, an elaborate "fort" built far back in the woods. There was the usual lookout perch in the upper branches of an enormous maple, a rope and rickety board bridge from the perch down to the main treehouse, a ground-level redoubt built of stone and roofed with steel that the wind had taken off the barn and a flagstone path that skirted the swampy moat. It was a place in which to dream, not an adult place, and so I left it as it was and didn't interfere. I only hope that the dreamers found as much joy in the fort as I have remembering the days when they raced the goats to the foot of the hill and all tumbled together at the bottom.

For every family wonder, there were setbacks. Dangerously high fevers when the lane was choked with snow. Boring hours on school buses. Frustrations with the family taxi service, which was always too much for the adults and not enough for the children. Chores that city children wouldn't have. Pets that were fun but had to be fed every day. Worries about teenage drivers.

Sound familiar? I suspect that any city parent could compile a similar list of joys and frustrations and the balance wouldn't be much different.

CULTURAL
ILLUSIONS

▼▼▼▼▼

I turned on the radio Saturday afternoon to hear the Texaco broadcast "live from the Metropolitan Opera in New York." Music lovers don't need to be told, but the rest of you should know that the Texaco broadcast is an institution, older than *Front Page Challenge* and *I Love Lucy* combined.

The announcer began by saying that the star of the day's performance would be the world-renowned Kathleen Battle. He sketched the diva's illustrious career but neglected to mention her childhood. As it happens, Ms. Battle and I grew up in the same little backwater town. And I remember hearing the opera broadcasts in that forgotten backwater when the diva – and I – was much too young to even know where New York was.

The reason why I remember the Texaco broadcasts so vividly, from an age when Jack Benny or *The Shadow* loomed much larger in the cultural consciousness, is Mother. She always got a faraway look in her eyes when the Saturday-afternoon opera came on. It wasn't the music so much as the effect it had on her that made the lasting impression. It was a look that a youngster might see as a little bit sad, and it was just private enough that you didn't dare ask. She wasn't a true-blue opera fan. In fact, if there was a baseball game on the dial, Texaco didn't stand a chance. But opera had an aura about it that made us walk on tiptoes through the kitchen and leave her to her reverie.

Now that I'm older and more cynical – or more romantic – I can connect those mysterious Saturday afternoons with a story she sometimes told of her salad days, when she was slim and single and living much closer to the city. The story had to do with an invitation to a real opera, box seats, a borrowed dress and long, lacy gloves. It was the only opera she ever saw, but she never mentioned the name of the work or what it might have been about. Her tale dwelt, instead, on an untimely rip and the humiliation of exposure in the midst of the cultured crowd. Not the exposure of an innocent bit of skin but the exposure of a provincial girl who borrowed dresses and didn't fit in.

Not surprisingly, I came of age thinking that "culture," whatever it was, could only happen among well-dressed, consenting adults. And it was certainly confined to cities. Adult attempts to civilize us with music and dance and Latin declensions were doomed to wither on geography's cross. Like poor Mr. Chambers.

He was our newly imported music teacher. A long lock of chestnut hair fell across his face and had to be regularly swept aside with the back of his hand. It was the smoking, though, that really set him apart. Other teachers smoked, but in styles that fit the time and place. The science teacher smoked unfiltered Camels and left them in the corner of his mouth to let a perpetual curl of smoke annoy one eye shut and turn the side of his face to walnut. The English teacher smoked Luckies and, as a result of a war injury, could send puffs of smoke out his ears. He survived the Luckies and World War II only to die of a broken neck after falling out of a tree while chasing a raccoon. Anyway, the new music teacher smoked white filter tips that he pinched between thumb and end of forefinger – backwards! The lit end sticking up instead of cupped down in his hand. Talk about not fitting in! Determined to be the bearer of culture, he announced on his first day at the school that he would like to form a string orchestra. Any student with an instrument was invited to audition. The next morning, 17 eager pupils crowded into his room with 16 guitars and a banjo. That wasn't exactly what he had had in mind. He hung on for a few more years and then ran off with the flutist from the marching band. Fortunately for the future of opera, Kathleen Battle attended a different school.

Dancing school wasn't much more successful. Madam drilled us on the six basic steps that were already passé in the rest of the world. By the time we figured out dance cards and the fox-trot and worked up enough nerve to attempt the fancy bits, we had reached the fumbling peak of adolescence. I lost control of Nancy in the middle of a twirl and threw her spinning across a table of shy wallflowers and sticky soda pop. Looking back on the mess, I can see that it had very little to do with the place and lots to do with the age. The same sorts of things probably happened in downtown Paris. But that's not the way we saw it then. We believed that such awkwardness and uncertainty could not live in the city. Only country lives were nasty, brutish and interminably long. Only in the country would we have awful nicknames like Horsefoot, Clodhopper and Hammerhead. City lives were cultured and sophisticated.

Imbued with that delusion, we washed cars and sold pencils for one entire year to save enough to charter a bus and take the graduating class to New York City. Most of the academic year was dedicated to that purpose. Predictably, our attempts to blend into the highlife unnoticed weren't quite successful. Butch and Darrell bought a bottle of rum and started a party room. Somebody unfamiliar with radi-

127

ators backed out of the shower and into a steam pipe. Fabled Radio City, we discovered, was little more than a movie house, and we'd already seen the film back home. The Bowery wasn't that different from neighbourhoods in other places and not that different from Butch and Darrell's room. Still, this was the big time, and we were determined.

Mick and I bought some real silk ties for $2 and invited Nancy and Shirley to dinner. This would be the ultimate in sophisticated living, the final justification for all those pencils and dirty cars. Just like the movies. I had to promise Nancy that if there were dancing, I would not attempt to twirl her. We would all dress to a fault so that no one, not even the waiter, would be able to tell that we were imposters, provincials in disguise.

We chose a French restaurant in the mid-Forties because it had an awning over the entrance. Inside, it was everything we had hoped it would be: white tablecloths, candles and a nearly full house of much older sophisticates dressed as well as we hoped we were. And it was a couple of things that we had hoped it wouldn't be: more silverware than we knew how to use and a menu that none of us could read. An imperious, black-tailed waiter swept down upon us like a vulture, bent slightly at the waist and blinked. We panicked. Too late to leave, blind to looming poverty, we ordered steak, pheasant, anything we could think of that sounded expensive enough to be on a menu that fat and foreign. The ruse worked – he wrote it all down and glided away.

The only thing that set us apart, at first, was our little island of silence. We spoke to one another in whispers, afraid some little slip would give us away. People at the other tables clinked and laughed out loud as if they ate there every night. We were sure they did.

We got through the soup all right and didn't really come apart until the first course of solid food. The soup spoon had been obvious, but the array of forks unnerved poor Shirley, and she dithered and shook until the fork slipped out of her sweaty hand and onto the hardwood floor with a clatter. In the very instant that it hit the floor, every conversation in the place took a simultaneous breath. The clatter rang in the unexpected and elegant silence like a bus token in the collection plate. Eyes turned. Food stopped halfway to mouths. I looked down to see if my real silk tie had started to curl. Poor Shirley turned scarlet and did the only proper thing – she pretended nothing had happened. There were, after all, lots of other forks to choose from. Retrieving the lost one would only tell them who was guilty.

With our eyes on our plates, we didn't actually see the man coming, but we heard him. The noisy scrape of chair on wood from the other side of the room punctuated the silence that the fork had created. Then his steps, deliberate and just a little unsteady, weaving between the tables. He stopped beside Shirley with a deep, sweeping bow. A middle-aged man in a three-piece suit, too short to be dashing, too drunk to be debonair, he presented the awful fork with a flourish that could be seen from the Bronx.

"I believe you dropped your fork," he boomed. Shirley pretended it wasn't happening. I could feel my zits beginning to glow beneath the Clearasil. My steam-pipe burn began to throb.

"I said," he repeated, "you dropped your fork!" I dared to look around, hoping he might be addressing some other table behind us. He wasn't. On the other side of the room, a middle-aged woman glowered at us all. She was alone. The chair opposite her had been pushed away. There was a napkin on the floor beside it.

Shirley accepted the fork. "You're cute," he said. "Where are you from?" Titters ran through nearby tables.

Then, somewhere on the other side of the room, another fork clattered to the floor.

"What's your name?" the sophisticate persisted. Another fork hit the floor. And another. Our visitor, not taking his eyes off Shirley, tossed his head toward the sound of the forks. "My wife," he explained. "She's an old crow."

More forks – crash clatter clatter – coming closer now as the abandoned wife began to aim. He straightened up and looked back from where he had come. "Caw, Caw, Caw!" he called. "Caw, Caw, Caw!"

We escaped unscathed but not unchanged. Never again could we be cowed by the city. The tiniest whiff of urban pretension or of presumed sophistication takes me back to that night in New York when our provincial inferiority complex was stripped bare, tested and then discarded.

Living in crowded places, we learned, does not necessarily create good taste or good manners. The slobs and the snobs are everywhere.

THE GEOGRAPHY OF CULTURE

Manners, however, are little more than the parsley on culture's plate. The central questions are: What is culture? And can it live in the country?

To be fair, let us take the broadest definition and include all of the good things that society creates for itself: good books, good music, good films, good food, sports, cabaret, dancing and even television. Add more if you like. We won't try to pin it down too tightly or insist upon "best" rather than "good," because that presumes some unity of taste which does not exist — which should not exist in an interesting world. Let's look, instead, for variety.

Variety not only assumes some tolerance of wider tastes, it also admits some borrowing from one society to another. Thus, New York's finest dining does not insist on only genuine New York pastrami and coneys (thank God) but borrows freely from French, Chinese and Armenian cuisine — and from anybody else who makes good food.

And before we go on to say where culture is, let's extend our definition of what it is to one more essential distinction: culture includes those who consume it as well as those who produce it. This is important, because those who paint, compose, cook, dance or throw baseballs well don't have to be in the same physical place as those who look, listen, eat and cheer. Not anymore. Thanks, Texaco.

The cultural classics — literature, drama, music, dance and art — could, in theory, take place anywhere. In practice, those arts have been held captive in the grand buildings that housed them. The biggest libraries, galleries, theatres, museums and concert halls were concentrated in the biggest cities. The audiences went to the biggest buildings, and the performers went to the audiences.

There have been some natural, historic reasons for the concentration of cultural buildings. The obvious one is that the big buildings were expensive. No society could afford a major opera hall in every village and town. Demagogues centralized cultural houses for the greater amusement of king and court. Democrats did the same in the interest of spending public money where the most voters lived. The result was the same: One or two cities in every country ended up with the bulk of the cultural facilities.

Facilities — not necessarily functions. Bricks and mortar do not make music. To say that some grand city is a cultural centre because the biggest buildings are there is as illogical as suggesting that New York is a more religious place than Lethbridge, Alberta, because it has a bigger cathedral; or, conversely, dismissing Lethbridge as a spiritual desert because it has smaller churches. In the real world, what goes on in the building quickly becomes captive to economics. Big buildings have big expenses and need big audiences to fill them.

130

And big is not necessarily synonymous with discerning or with variety. Big means always going for the sure bet, for mass appeal. That's why Broadway prefers long-running pap to the more lively variety of experiments that appear off Broadway. In Canada, exciting theatre has come from Codco, Neptune and Theatre Passe Muraille, while the giant stages of Toronto are stuck with *Cats* and *The Best Little Whorehouse in Texas*.

The economics of "big" attracts artists and performers as well as bricks and mortar to the city. But the same logic controls the result. "Big" demands mass-appeal performances. And it demands the same of performers. It demands older, better-known names. Lively variety, unproven experiments, new ideas and young performers must serve their apprenticeships on smaller stages in the city and in smaller places. Which suits the smaller places just fine. Smaller stages get the vigour and variety of creative beginnings, and the grand halls get Victor Borge and Jean Stapleton. Victor Borge and Jean Stapleton we can watch on television.

A couple of weeks ago, the Caravan Stage Company came rumbling down the road in swaying wagons drawn by Clydesdale horses. The washtubs, bikes and paraphernalia of family life came along, lashed to the tops and sides of the wagons. The actors were driving the teams and riding behind on the spare horses. I pulled off the road while they passed. The hand-lettered sign on the side of one of the wagons announced two performances at the local fairgrounds.

And so, on the following night, we took a blanket and went to the theatre. We arrived just minutes before curtain time and had to park almost 50 yards away from the tent that was raised on the grass between the wagons. In that distance, we passed two child actors helping one another with makeup and two older players by the side of the road locked in a heated dispute over the nuances of a scene from the play we were about to see.

The Lions Club members, equipped with canvas money aprons, were selling tickets by the open flap of the tent. Inside, a few rows of plank benches curved around the open stage. The open space behind the benches filled with people who had thought to bring along their lawn chairs. The strip of grass between the benches and the stage filled with younger kids and couples sitting on the ground. We might have squeezed in a few more around the five-piece orchestra, but let's call it a full house at about 200 people.

The play was called *Stealing Home*. It's about Nicaraguan baseball, about imperialism and being in love, the lure of the dollar and trying to decide where you belong in the world. It's political and musical, funny and earnest. The little kids laughed at all the wrong places, the parents squirmed when the whore struggled to climax with the impotent baseballer, and we all had a wonderful time.

If *Stealing Home* ever plays Broadway, you'll sit as far from the stage as I parked, the delightful Latin pitcher will be played by Don Johnson, the whore will control herself, the raw politics will be censored to avoid offending anyone, it will cost $50 instead of $5, you'll have to get tickets six months in advance instead of five minutes, and you won't be allowed to walk through the backstage arguments on the way to your seat.

To be fair, some things will be better in New York. There won't be any mosquitoes sneaking past the flap of the tent, and the plush seats will be a little more comfortable than the planks. But I can't think of any other advantages. I was going to add that in New York, you won't have to bring a blanket to ward off the late-night chill, but then I remembered how nice it was to snuggle under the blanket with Liz, and I moved that item to the list of things the New York audience will miss.

Those who create the arts do tend to end their careers in the city, serving the larger economy in the larger buildings. But the beginnings of artistic endeavour are, in fact, more widely spread. They don't all have tents and horses, but literature, music and the visual arts display some of the same patterns of increased provincial vigour.

THANKS, GUTENBERG

Alice Munro and Margaret Laurence lived and worked in small-town Ontario. Robertson Davies launched his literary career from Peterborough. Alberta's Aritha Van Herk, British Columbia's Susan Musgrave, Alden Nowlan from New Brunswick . . . the American scene is little different. The publishing houses may be concentrated in Toronto and New York, but the creativity comes from smaller places. Romantic ideas of salon days or the movable literary feast of 1920s' Paris have no modern equivalent. Today's literary "scene" is dispersed worldwide. García Márquez from Aracataca, Colombia; Naipaul from Chaguanas, Trinidad; Gordimer, Solzhenitsyn, Vargas Llosa . . . the production of literature has decentralized.

The consumption of literature is even more decentralized than its production. There is no reason whatsoever that one must live in the city in order to be well read. Quality bookstores may be scarce in little towns, but they aren't that common in the city either. What advantage is there in having 50 bookstores if 49 of them carry the same selection of paperback best-sellers and diet books? Any town with a single bookstore is big enough to allow its citizens to be well read. The store will order any book in print – all you have to do is ask. You really don't even need the store. All it takes is a mailbox to subscribe to journals or a membership in a book club.

If you don't have a mailbox, you can still borrow almost any book in the world from the smallest rural library. I know, I know, the little libraries don't always have much on the shelves, but they do have access to the vast network of interlibrary loans, government documents, periodicals and reference indexes. And, no matter how small, public libraries are almost always eager to help. The staff of the library and archives in Vernon, British Columbia, spent hours digging out old photographs and newspapers and contacting amateur historians to help me track down some 19th-century minutiae. The Ripley, Ohio, library is a gold mine of details on the underground railroad. And a minuscule township library turned up just the volume I needed on the second law of thermodynamics; mind you, it was shelved with the fiction in the librarian's belief that nonfiction had hard covers and fiction came in paperback. But we overlooked the fine points and delighted in the service.

On occasion, I have forgotten and assumed that the city service must be better because it's bigger. A mistake. The last time, I needed a particular book by a *New York Times* columnist. It was a recent edition and the author enjoys a popular following, so it would seem an easy find. Nevertheless, I travelled to the capital to try the big library. The book wasn't in the catalogue.

"No," said the librarian, "if it's not in the catalogue, we don't have it."

"It's fairly new," I said. "Perhaps it's on order."

"Not likely," she answered. "We're not ordering many new books this year. It's the budget. But I'll check."

The budget. As she said it, she rolled her head around to take in the whole expanse of oak and tile that makes the newish building beautiful. Remember, readers, that careful distinction between the building and the function which it houses? Here it is again.

"Not on order," she says. "Would you like me to try interlibrary loans?"

I would. She did. And the book arrived a few days later from the little library in Sault Ste. Marie, 495 miles away. As it happens, I've used that little library in the Soo, and I know that apart from having the new book I needed, the one the capital couldn't afford, the Soo library is a delightful place to work. The big lake steamers glide past the windows on quiet afternoons, and it's all as serene as the reading salon of an ocean liner. Any book in the world you want, and atmosphere too. No big city offers better access to literature than this.

THANKS, EDISON

Music, like literature, is a pleasure available to all, no matter where you live. Recorded music comes to the living room at a fraction of the ticket price. Tapes and especially compact discs allow a quality of sound at least as good as the concert hall. If you discount the coughers and programme rustlers in a typical concert audience, the quality of the music may be better in your living room.

Although regional festivals and travelling companies visit smaller towns and villages, the biggest live performances do happen more often in the city. The question is whether that matters to the music lover. Do you need to see the music as well as hear it?

A treasured friend subscribes to box seats for the symphony season. Whenever she can't attend, we get the unused tickets and drive to the city for music in the flesh. I love it. But I couldn't help making two observations.

The first is an elderly lady who sits just behind "our" box, in the first row of balcony seats. When the concert begins, she closes her eyes and enters some more private musical reverie, nodding and swaying ever so slightly. Only once did she snore out loud. But – even assuming she's awake in there – it made me wonder whether the music, unlike little children, should be heard and not seen. Which led to the second, entirely unscientific observation. I take off my glasses. Now, instead of bow ties, hair partings and flying fingers, the visual part of the concert is a soft kaleidoscope of flashing brass and varnished planes of wood. Those of you who remember the 1960s might liken the effect to recreational chemistry. Seeing less actually seems to enhance the music. The fewer details I see, the more nuances I hear. Don't ask me why. Maybe it has something to do with the kind of sensory concentration that causes lovers to close their eyes while they are kissing. Anyway, try it. Then ask yourself if you really need a concert hall nearby in order to enjoy the music.

Frans is a tall, quiet Dutchman whose tastes have been refined by almost 50 years of travel. He's lived in Paris and Kathmandu. "But," he admits, "the most sublime moment of my life was playing Bach on the piano while a snowstorm raged outside the window." The piano, the window and the storm were in majestic concert at the end of a steep, isolated, rutted road, several forests and valleys removed from urban concert halls. Frans saw nothing beyond the black glass but driven snow. He didn't feel the need for a crowd in order to enjoy the music.

By the logic of bricks and mortar, the big art galleries and museums, too, are concentrated in the cities. Does it matter? And do you have to live in the city to enjoy the best of art and archaeology?

The creators of culture paint and carve and weave just about anywhere. There is no real need to concentrate such activity in crowded places. Moreover, in societies like ours, where the creators are valued somewhat less than plumbers and are as gnats on the back of economic giants like orthodontists, it is inevitable that the artist is sometimes compelled to live and work outside the city, where life is more affordable. Painters might say that the light is better, and writers might use the excuse of peace and quiet, but the simple fact is that rural economics are more amenable to the meagre income of art. The old artistic garret has long since been sandblasted and skylighted for lawyers and dentists. Young artists who are willing to starve for the sake of tradition, and old artists who might finally be collecting their dues, might live in the urban studios, but much of the production of contemporary art is a rural phenomenon.

For cultural consumers, the city museums and galleries do perform one function that smaller regional museums cannot perform as well: they collect a vast variety of things. Regional museums have specific depth; big-city museums have general breadth. Thus, if you're interested in seeing a superb display of coal-mining history – tools, miners' lives, labour politics and anything else connected with that industry – there is no better museum than the one in little Glace Bay, Nova Scotia. By contrast, the much bigger Canadian Museum of Civilization in Ottawa has a tiny fraction of the display put on by the Glace Bay museum. In the Museum of Civilization, visitors walk through one small room that has been modelled as an ersatz mining shaft. In Glace Bay, visitors go down an actual shaft. Depth versus breadth. The Museum of Civilization, unlike Glace Bay, must also give display space to farming tools, immigrant history, a stuffed buffalo, a plastic igloo, and so on.

When the children were preschoolers, they loved it. They ran from the dinosaurs to the igloo to the stuffed moose and were ready for the canteen and the bathroom before the adults had time to read a plaque. Now that they've been down a real coal mine, seen a real moose and crawled inside a real igloo (all in the country), a visit to a city museum seems pretty pale stuff.

Big museums collect things from the countryside and put them all together in one big expensive place. That's fine for those who want to see a little bit of a lot of things, like channel hopping on a satellite dish. And if you live in Ontario, it might be interesting to see one small room done up like a Cape Breton coal mine. But if you live in Cape Breton, you've likely seen better at home.

One more example. When the children were younger, we lived without any indoor plumbing. There was an old cast-iron hand pump outside the back door that served as the sole water source. At least once a year, we drove into the city to visit museums and galleries. A special favourite was a particularly fine museum of science and technology. Frankly, one of its attractions was that we were rarely bothered by crowds – even on school holidays. The hordes of city children fought for peeking room at the chick incubator and lined up to pump water from the old-fashioned pump. Ours ran right by the crowds to see the electricity display and the trains. Who wants to pump water from a dumb old pump anyway? That's for city kids.

BRICKS AND MORTAR

Now a concession. I've argued that some of the arts are as accessible in the country as they are in the city. But there is one aspect of classic culture that is harder to find in the country, and that is major stage performances: drama, opera and dance. It's not impossible. Perth, with its 6,000 people, supports a resident summer theatre company plus three or four more touring performances through the year. Banff has a major arts festival. So do Stratford, Charlottetown, Niagara-on-the-Lake and many others. But sustained, large-scale stage productions are still mostly a city privilege.

It is, however, a matter of degree. My urban friends make four errors when they suggest that it's a cultural desert outside the city limits. That's not what they actually say. What they actually say is the other side of that assumption: "I prefer the city because there are so many things going on . . . because I enjoy music or film or theatre or whatever." What they are really saying is that they can't imagine those things exist outside the city. Here's what they overlook:

First, they don't distinguish between portable culture and those other things which do demand big stages, big audiences, lots of bricks and mortar. Gutenberg started printing books more than 500 years ago, and yet some still cannot accept that literature is portable. The big-city library may borrow its books from Sault Ste. Marie, but because the building is bigger, the urbanites drive by and somehow come to equate their concrete with culture. Similarly with music. The CBC and American public radio can deliver the finest classical music to the most isolated backwoods cabin. And they do. Listen to the requests from Goose Bay, Happy Valley and Flin Flon. You don't have to have a ticket to hear the music anymore.

Second, the urbophiles too easily overlook the cultural activity that does take place outside the city limits: writing, painting, acting, playing. Performances are smaller, the artists younger, the work is often less well known; sometimes it is worse than what can be seen in the city; sometimes it's better, or at least more fun.

Third, my urban friends use their cultural facilities much less often than they imagine. Quick now, how many times a year do you actually attend the opera? The symphony? The ballet? The statistics suggest that if you are an average Canadian, you will attend the theatre about once every four years, other live performances (opera, dance or music) about once every 7½ years. Even films, available everywhere, aren't that popular: four a year is the average.

Fourth, and finally, my friends don't understand that when culture cannot be moved, people can. Country people can and do visit the city for pleasure and enlightenment, just as city people occasionally drive beyond the limits to enjoy a mountain or a lake. Torontonians happily drive for hours to ski yet still find it hard to imagine that those who live in the mountains might live culturally rich lives by travelling the same distance to Toronto for those bricks-and-mortar events that won't come to them.

Call it the urban cottage, a special retreat to those things not easily available at home, wherever home is. Urbanites retreat to the lake, country people have a weekend on the town — same thing. We provincials might have to drive a few hours to see a ballet, just as urbanites might drive a few hours to see a tree that's not tied down.

POPULAR CULTURE

Television, films, books, magazines and recorded music reach the countryside with precisely the same speed and substance that urbanites enjoy. By the numbers, our cultural lives are essentially equal 97 percent of the time. That's the percentage of time we spend on print and electronic cultures that don't care where we live. Even the final 3 percent – that 1½ hours a week that we spend attending movies, live performances and spectator sports – isn't all that different in the country and the city. The movies are the same, the games are the same, and the live performances include many more popular entertainments than things like ballet that rarely move out of the city.

That geographic indifference of popular electronic culture wasn't always the case. And it is that old perception of disparity which colours urban ideas of the rural cultural desert. Cultural deprivation isn't what it used to be.

In 1965, I spent a summer in the Simpson Desert with a seismographic crew. There were 15 of us in metal huts, camped on an arid plain so barren that the tallest feature on the horizon was a lump of wild camel dung (cross my heart). The company's idea of recreation was to fly out a load of beer and rum on the regular Friday-afternoon supply plane. That lasted until about 2 o'clock Saturday morning. Then we had the rest of the week to amuse ourselves – when we weren't too busy sweating and blowing holes in the sand.

For 6½ days a week, week after week after week, mental and cultural stimulation was based entirely on a battery-operated record player and a 35mm slide projector. Oh yes, there was one James Bond novel with the last 10 pages torn out; but after you had read that and guessed at the ending a couple of times, it really came down to the records and the slides.

The man who owned the slide projector took pictures only of the desert. When he went away on leave, he was much too busy for photography. The man with the record player had brought only two records with him: a 45 rpm Elvis single and a Rolf Harris album that was warped with heat and scratched with sand. Rolf Harris (of *Tie Me Kangaroo Down* fame) wasn't all that much better than looking at pictures of the desert.

We alternated: Monday, Wednesday and Saturday, we listened to the two records; Tuesday, Thursday and Sunday, we watched the slides of the desert. *That* was cultural deprivation.

Now when the kids say, "Daaad, there's nothing to dooo," I tell them about the slides and the two records, until they're as sick of the story as we were of Rolf Harris and "This is a sand dune, and this is us listening to Rolf Harris, and this is a piece of camel dung . . . think we'll turn in now."

Today, even bush camps have satellite dishes and VCRs (though I wonder if the guys coming back from leave ever remember to bring new tapes).

The past 20 years have brought two enormous changes to the way all of us share in the culture. The first change is the very obvious, visible change in the way culture is delivered – the electronic revolution. Electronic delivery widens access for everyone. The second change springs from the first – wider access and more variety loosen the old monopoly at the centre and decentralize control.

The electronic revolution in popular culture goes far beyond satellites and VCRs. The technology touches everything. Take something as hidebound and traditional as a newspaper, for example. It still has big pages, small print, headlines, a mix of news and advertising. But look a little more closely. Offset printing has put more colour and better photography into the news. Electronic keyboards with modem links from any news site in the world make coverage wider and faster. Production changes allow newspapers like *The Globe and Mail* to write the story on the other side of the world, edit it in Toronto, print it in another city and sell it in the local village store by 10 o'clock in the morning. Toronto's significance in the far-flung process is diminished. The newspaper responds by printing less Toronto news, more wire-service stories and syndicated features. The city, as a necessary centre, is less relevant than it was.

Music, in the popular culture, has been swept by similar changes. Like the news, it has lost its former geographic centres. As record producers synthesize more and more of the sounds, the actual musicians become less significant in the process. Whole schools of artists who once congregated to experiment and build musical traditions that were specific to a city, or even to a neighbourhood, have been dispersed. There's still jazz on Bourbon Street, but it's played, recorded and heard all over the world. A 17-year-old neighbour created some jazz in my kitchen the other night. He tapped out a simple, one-finger melody on an electronic keyboard, recorded it, repeated it with variations that he added with the touch of a few buttons, gave each round a different instrumental voice, then syncopated the whole concoction with a rhythm key. He had a whole roomful of instruments and recording equipment in a single device that fit in his coat pocket. He's never been to New Orleans in his life.

There was a time when Saturday night in rural places meant listening to radio music from the city – from the Stardust Ballroom or the beautiful Waldorf-something-or-other in New York. The musicians and the dancers and the glamour were there. Listening always brought a little pang of having missed it – of being outside the light. It was like listening to a grown-up party through the floor register, lying in pyjamas in an upstairs hall. When I grow up, I'll stay up all night or live in New York and dance at the Stardust Ballroom.

Age undermined the wish to stay up all night, and electronics destroyed the idea of musical meccas. If there is still a Stardust Ballroom, the odds are that the dancers are moving to recorded music, music which was recorded in Dublin and synthesized into something entirely different somewhere in Tennessee. The centre is gone.

When the wellspring of all popular music seemed to be Liverpool, the audiences and imitators didn't all flock to Liverpool to be part of the excitement. The excitement spread electronically. I heard it in northern Canada, in Tasmania and in a Philippine peasant hut. It was a house of thatch and split bamboo built on stilts. There was no electricity and no furniture. I slept on a floor of woven mats and woke in the middle of the night to the sound of the water buffalo stirring under the hut, and to the sound of the Beatles.

"What's that?" I whispered in the dark.

"Beatles," replied my host, as if I were some kind of cultural moron and he were the host of the Stardust Ballroom.

"But where's the music coming from?"

"Transistor," he replied matter-of-factly from somewhere in the dark, on the other side of the bamboo screen, above the water buffalo, between the wide paddies of rice still black in the unwired countryside. What did Liverpool matter?

Easier access is only half of the cultural revolution, however. The new technology has not only made the city less essential to the consumption of culture, it has decentralized the production of culture. When Gutenberg printed his Bible, he took religion away from the church and put it in the hands of every literate person. Printing decentralized knowledge. It made access easier because there were more Bibles available. But it also made it easier to produce books, and a wider variety of books got written. It wasn't just more Bibles, it was other books that explained the Bible, that contradicted the Bible, that dashed off into realms of ideas that had nothing to do with the Bible.

So, too, today. When satellite and cable opened every corner of the continent to television transmission, it meant that rural homes had the same cultural giant in the living room as city families had. But that was only the beginning of the revolution. It would go on to decentralize the medium itself.

Television in the 1960s was three American and two Canadian networks. The entire North American television culture was controlled by five big corporations. It was produced in the cities for a city audience. Even those productions with rural settings or rural themes were filtered through a centralized urban view of what rural life was like. So we got *The Beverly Hillbillies* and then *The Waltons*.

Network production is still an urban love affair with itself, but now there are dozens of alternatives: news channels, sports, religion, education, movies, children's programming, other-language and regional networks. More importantly, every crossroad big enough for cable service has some local programming. Every family with a video camera can put itself on television. Decentralization doesn't just give us easier access to *The Waltons*. It also gives us a much wider variety of things to watch and a chance to join the producers. The city – the erstwhile centre – is no longer essential to the medium.

Other forms of popular culture have undergone a similar process of diversification and decentralization.

Magazines used to be urban monsters with huge circulations and mass appeal. Now technology allows the publishers to identify smaller, more specialized audiences, attract specific advertisers for that audience, then print and deliver just about anywhere. *Life* and *Look* have given way to *Runner's World, Ballet News, Cottage Life, Canadian Workshop* and hundreds and hundreds of other special-interest publications. We no longer have to write and read about only those broad – usually urban – themes that enjoy mass appeal.

While some large newspapers have monopolized urban markets and then expanded to serve national audiences with more general coverage, the bottom end of the market has blossomed with a very different kind of expansion. Small-town weeklies, even neighbourhood newsletters and flyers, have prospered. Some of the same technology that enables a large publisher to spread across a continent also allows a desk-top publisher to serve a small audience that would have been ignored just a few years ago. Local weeklies have changed to offset printing, syndicated features and "spin-off" specialty publications for bridal season, tourist season and advertising themes.

Cinema audiences have left the huge picture palaces, where Hollywood blockbusters once played for weeks at a time. Now the trend is to multiscreen complexes, where the same-size audience divides itself to watch six different films in six smaller rooms. That might not mean much to urban film-goers, who have always had choices. But in smaller cities, the faster turnover of more films means much more variety.

In every realm of popular culture, the trend has been to easier access, decentralized controls and a wider variety for the consumer. The greatest impact of this revolution is outside the cities. Country life, quite simply, has changed radically in the last 20 years. Small places now have immediate access to the larger popular culture, and they now have the means to develop local cultural interests.

RECREATION

Finally, let's lump together all the other things that people do for fun and test the old urban assumption that the countryside is dull and the city is where "it" is happening. Is it?

What do urbanites really do with their spare time? One 1981 time-use study suggests that rural and metropolitan settings make little difference in the time budgets and daily routines of Canadians. Urbanites spend 5.34 hours a day on spare-time activities compared with 5.06 hours a day for rural dwellers. The surprise is that urbanites are more passive in their leisure activities, rural dwellers more active. Urbanites do spend more time visiting friends (12 minutes), but they also spend more time driving to their activities (13 minutes more).

Activity	Metropolitan	Rural
	(Mean hours daily)	
Participation in organizations	0.20	0.22
Entertainment (visiting friends)	1.01	0.81
Active leisure	0.81	0.95
Passive leisure	3.32	3.08

142

Urbanites might find it hard to believe the numbers, perhaps because it's hard to think of themselves as stay-at-homes when they can see all that exciting nightlife advertised in the city papers. The city undoubtedly does offer more possibilities for recreation and entertainment. But possibilities don't count unless you participate. If the average Canadian sees one play every four years, then it doesn't really matter very much where he or she lives. A little town like Perth stages 20 times more theatre than the average person attends.

Rural people won't be surprised to see that their leisure time is more active than urban leisure. Every crossroad in Canada has a ball diamond and a rink and a slate of teams looking for players. Outdoor sports – swimming, skiing, hiking, fishing, hunting, boating – are more accessible in the country than in the city. Within a 15-minute drive, I can bowl, ski, curl, sail, windsurf, water-ski, golf, play squash, racquetball, tennis, baseball, football, broomball, hockey, badminton or volleyball. There's no luge track around, and the polo scene is pretty quiet, but nearly everything else is at hand – close, affordable and convenient.

The volleyball is a good illustration of the way things happen outside the city. It is, simply, a case study in practical anarchy at work. The group, if I can call it that, doesn't have a name, a sponsor or a slate of officers. It isn't registered with any recreation association or government body. It doesn't have a constitution, membership or dues. Here's how it works: every Tuesday night at 7 o'clock, 10 to 20 players show up at the local school gymnasium. You put a dollar in the envelope lying on the stage and play a little pickup basketball until the others arrive.

Any two people who feel like it choose the sides, and then play begins. We do keep score (after a fashion), though nobody is very fussy about the rules. The score really only serves to tell us when the game is over. Nobody keeps track of who won what, since the sides change every week. Indeed, if the score gets too lopsided, we swap players in the course of an evening to balance the odds.

In the past 10 years, the faces have changed – job transfers, babies and creeping age force some to drop out, and newcomers keep arriving. There are married couples and parent-child combinations. The regulars include a grandmother and a 14-year-old boy.

Play is spirited enough to send everybody home tired, but it is not competitive enough to cause fights or any injuries more serious than the odd bruise.

John Looby looks after the envelope and pays the rent for the gym. John, a building contractor by day, ended up with the envelope because he comes more regularly than most. There wasn't an election or even much of a discussion. The last keeper of the envelope missed a number of Tuesday nights, and trying to give him the money got to be a nuisance.

Nobody keeps an account of who has paid and how much ought to be in the kitty. It has never been too little to pay the rent, and that's all that matters. When the envelope gets too full, we declare a free night and nobody pays. At the end of the year, we blow the surplus on a party.

Parties? Music? Dancing? Again, the choices are limited, but there's more than enough action for any insomniac. The local weekly lists five area dances coming up this weekend. Three nearby hotels have bands. And those are just the advertised events. More often, it's the kind of thing Lisa organized last winter.

Lisa works in the hardware store. Her husband, Carl, is a stonemason. They live on the fringe of a little lakeside village that gets quiet when the summer people leave. Lisa got the winter blahs and organized a party for the whole community. She booked the lodge, called everybody she could think of, and we had a party: drinks around the fireplace first, a sit-down dinner for the hundred or so neighbours who came, then a clock presentation for Hazel and Eric who had just retired from the village store, a horse-drawn sleigh ride across the fields to a big bonfire and portable wine bar, then back to the lodge for dancing. There was some gentle teasing for Bev Hall, who blew up his boat last summer, and somebody tittered "fix" when Carl won one of Lisa's door prizes. But nobody threw forks or yelled "Caw, Caw, Caw" across the room. We're much too sophisticated for that sort of behaviour.

URBAN HICK

The first principle of ecology insists that everything is connected to everything else. Like hair spray and the ozone layer, chocolate and skin trouble. So, too, with town and country. The two aren't separate states, with a line at the city limits – sophisticates here and yokels over there. If it ever was that way in the past, it is no more. Urbanites eat rural-raised McBurgers, and farmers watch *Miami Vice*. Country people go to town to see ballet, and townsfolk drive outside the

144

limits to picnic on the grass. Any urbanite who feels complete sleeping, working, living and playing solely within the city is as stunted and parochial as the olden-day farmer who never went to town. The phenomenon is urban hick.

Reality has also reversed old notions of freedom and mobility. Former stereotypes pictured the rural dweller tied to the farm and to the narrow world of his birth, while the urbanite was thought to be mobile and free. No more. Now, some urbanites are effectively confined to work and residence by the sheer difficulty of getting anywhere else; some stay home for fear of unpleasantness in the streets and some for the simple fact that there is little pleasure in an evening stroll along the expressway.

There have been times and places when I might argue that the city is too expensive, too inconvenient and just no longer necessary for a full, happy cosmopolitan life. But I could never give it up entirely. That would make me as narrow-minded as the most intolerant townsman. That would almost make me a New Yorker. Gad!

And so, just to help me remember the nice things about the city, I made a special trip back to a special place. I meant to savour the best of it. I walked down a tree-lined street when the morning was fresh and watched a thousand beautiful young women make their way to work. I stopped to hear the street musicians, gave away spare change and lunched on hot, spicy sausage from a sidewalk cart. I browsed through the foreign press at the library. I even took joy in the anonymity and eavesdropped shamelessly on the stock tips and afternoon affairs that bubbled in a half-dark pub.

It was all very nice – for a little while. And then it began to pall. The birds – too uniformly grey – began to quarrel over crumbs. And the women who had smiled on their way to work pushed and crowded home at five. There was a nasty bit at the parking lot and some fender fencing on the freeway ramp.

Morning and evening were as different as an innocent flirtation and 15 years of bad marriage. And I didn't even have a city-sized mortgage to think about on my way home.

I can't pretend that the city doesn't still have some charms. And I will continue to use it in the same unfaithful way that city people use the lake and cottage. It's a nice place to visit, but I wouldn't want to live there.

DOMESTIC SCIENCE

▼▼▼▼▼

This is where the myth about the "simple" life in the country comes apart. It used to be simple. It might still be simple for some. But the truly simple life is in the city.

The average urban dweller is the blissfully ignorant beneficiary of a vast complex of engineering that brings water to the tap, takes it away from the toilet bowl, delivers the fuel, heats the home and carries away the garbage. That's the simple life. The systems that support such ease aren't simple, but that doesn't concern the urbanite. The urbanite isn't concerned or even aware, unless one of those systems happens to fail. And then the answer is simple: Call the landlord or the plumber. Or, in the event of profound failure, call city hall. That's as complex as urban life has to get: Set the thermostat, put the blue stuff in the toilet, and, in an emergency, dial the phone and complain.

The rural dweller has to know how to run all the complex systems that the urbanite merely uses. The private utilities that serve one rural home are, admittedly, smaller than the city utilities, but they aren't much simpler. And the rural dweller can't call city hall to complain that the water tastes funny.

He can call the pump repairman or one of a number of miscellaneous fix-its. But these are rarely as fast, as cheap or as reliable as the maintenance man in the basement apartment. Those who live beyond the end of the city pipes and services soon learn that the only choice is to learn a little domestic science.

WATER

The idea is simple enough: You drill a hole in the ground, water seeps into the hole from subterranean sources, a pump draws the water into the house and stores it in a pressure tank. You open the tap, and the water runs until pressure drops low enough to switch on the pump again to restore that pressure. That's just about what happens in an urban water system, except that the city adds a filtration/purification plant.

And therein lies the first and potentially most serious failure in a one-house water system: pollution. The home well relies on the soil to filter out impurities as the water percolates from the surface down to the water table. If surface water gets directly into the well, if the soil can't filter out the guck or if the water table carries impurities from some distant source, then the home waterworks has a problem.

148

It isn't an uncommon problem. Even in the pristine-appearing countryside, seepage from agricultural chemicals, nearby septic tanks and long-abandoned dumps can affect the water quality.

All of those problems and more can also affect city water. But the city dweller has government experts and scientists from lobby groups to worry about what's in the Great Lakes or the Mississippi and whether it's safe to drink. The rural dweller, by contrast, is expected to be responsible for his own healthy water. The power for political action to force long-term cleanup is in the city. The means for individual self-protection are limited.

Testing is an obvious step but a partial one at best. Local jurisdictions (county, town or region) have public health departments. Most of these have a standard, often free, service for testing wells. You may be given a plastic bottle and printed instructions on how to take the sample. You return the sample to the department, and they tell you whether the water meets local standards. The problem is that the local standard may only consider bacterial pollutants or those with fecal origins. That's important stuff, mind you, especially if there are neighbours and septic tanks nearby. But it's by no means the limit of all that can be in the water.

There are a few commercial laboratories that will test for other things, but always at a price and only for selected contaminants.

You tell them what you think is in the water, and they tell you whether it is there and in what quantity. If you do suspect something specific, by all means ask the health department to refer you to a reliable testing service.

The difficult part is knowing what to suspect. A well in farming country might be suspected of having at least a few of the common agricultural chemicals. Nearby factories might suggest other chemicals. Runoff from roads could carry lead, salt or herbicide residues. It isn't always so obvious, though. Take the case of the Blumers.

The Blumers moved from the city to a long-abandoned farm. "Long-abandoned" was part of its appeal. The farm had never been modern enough or successful enough for the fields to be treated with anything stronger than cow manure. It centred on the highest ground around – there could be no runoff from anything but themselves. They eschewed the three existing wells and drilled a brand-new one, far from the road and high above it. They drilled through solid rock, 76 feet into the water table, then added steel casing and a sealed cap before any nasties could get in from the surface. The taste was as cold and sweet as water could be. The health department gave it a perfect score. Then a mining van rolled up the lane, and the young geologist at the wheel asked if she could have a little water. The immediate response was social.

"Sure, help yourself." It wasn't a cold drink the stranger wanted, though. She took out sample bottles and a clipboard.

"What are you sampling for?" asked the Blumers, just a little taken aback.

"Radioactivity." She said it so matter-of-factly that it took a moment to sink in.

"You're kidding," they said, breathing out but not in.

"No, really. There's uranium all around here. We're just trying to find out where the concentrations are heavy enough to mine."

"Right here? On this farm?"

"We'll let you know." They never did let the Blumers know. Which gave some little solace that at least they weren't being irradiated in commercially viable quantities.

Small comfort, but instructive. The Blumers did take the three most important steps: They sought the least likely site for pollution (high ground, far from contaminating sources and known prior use), they took care to seal out surface water with casing and a cap, and they had the obvious testing done. Beyond that, we're all at risk.

Off-the-shelf solutions to water problems are widely advertised, but they aren't the panaceas that some of the makers claim. About half the water-treatment systems sold in Canada work with an activated carbon filter. At their best, these units do remove more than the frog spawn and silt that we see as visible pollutants. A carbon filter can also reduce the levels of organic chemicals, including chlorine, chloroform, pesticides and industrial chemicals.

Unfortunately, the cure isn't complete and doesn't last. Effectiveness decreases with use. Organic matter trapped in the filter can become a breeding ground for more bacteria. You'll have to change the cartridges frequently. And you'll have to remember that this system (and the newer reverse-osmosis systems) should be used only on water that has already been cleaned of microbes. Which means that you may have to add another unit to disinfect. Distillation, chlorination, ceramic candles, ozone, iodine and ultraviolet are all used to disinfect, but only distillation is effective against all pathogens. Ceramic candles, for example, remove protozoan cysts but not viruses, while chlorination may kill viruses but not protozoan cysts.

The only intelligent course is to test the water for any suspected pollutants. If necessary, add a treatment system designed specifically for that type of pollutant. Maintain the system religiously, and retest the water regularly.

Don't let the complications discourage you. Remember that most cities filter the flotsam and then add chlorine to kill the bacteria. The exotic, less visible impurities stay in the water. If it were as easy as installing a universal filter under the sink, they could put a big one under Niagara Falls and a couple of other key places and quit worrying about urban water quality.

In some areas, the groundwater carries dissolved minerals. These end up as rust stains in the tub or lime deposits in the kettle. The water may taste fine and be safe to drink, but the slow buildup of mineral sludge can cause a coronary in the dishwasher. Water softeners, in contrast to filters, aren't aimed at the health of the inhabitants but at the health of the plumbing. The softener takes the minerals out of the water before it reaches the taps and appliances. If the soap doesn't lather the way it should, you may have a mineral problem.

DIVINE GUIDANCE

If you're building in the country, one of the first decisions is where to dig or drill the well. There will be no shortage of advice from passersby. Before you take any of it seriously, remember this: Water divining, or "witching," is a matter of faith; some believe and some don't. If your first question upon meeting a stranger is, "What's your sign?" then by all means ask around for the local diviner and enjoy the show. Otherwise, ask the building contractor or the neighbours what the average local well depth is and how many dry holes are hit. At the same time, ask your local health inspector or building inspector what rate of flow will be sufficient for your family, your appliances and your shower habits.

You could ask the drilling contractor about well depth, but if you're enough of a skeptic to refuse the diviner, you'll be skeptic enough to figure out that drilling contractors charge by the foot – the deeper the well, the more they can charge. Think about it.

In fact, geology is most apt to spread the water around with broad strokes. It is possible to have a skinny little aquifer here – where the diviner's rod dips – and dry holes all around. But if the neighbour on one side has a 60-foot well at his back door and the neighbour on the other side has a 60-foot well at her back door, then the odds say that you'll hit water at 60 feet by your back door, wherever you position the house.

If you like, you can increase the depth of the well to improve the rate of flow. It is not, after all, an underground lake you're drilling into. It is porous rock or subsoil, saturated to a certain level with water. When you drill into the rock, water seeps from the sides of the shaft and fills the well to the top of the saturation level. When you pump water out, the level in the shaft drops until it reaches some equilibrium with the water seeping back in. Some strata of rock are more saturated than others. There may be water in the upper strata, but with a slow rate of seepage that won't allow you to pump a lot out quickly without temporarily emptying the shaft. The deeper the shaft, the more seepage there is to replace the water as it's pumped out.

In dry times, the entire water table drops. You can continue to pump water only as long as the well is deep enough and the pump strong enough to pull water from that depth. When you have rural neighbours, it is prudent to consider what other demands might be made on the shared water source. If the neighbours irrigate, for example, you should ask what happens to nearby wells in dry years. Then plan well depth and pump size accordingly. When the drillers arrive, you can ask them to stop at a predetermined depth to check the rate of flow. If it isn't adequate, they can drill a little farther and check again. Unless you're an orthodontist, it would probably pay to take the day off work and be there to insist that the drillers stop when the flow is sufficient. There are a lot of busy people with very deep, very expensive wells.

Where to drill is the question we avoided in the clash between magic and geology. The practical aspects are these: The pipe from well to house must be covered to keep it from freezing, and the well itself must be accessible for repair. That suggests putting the well as close to the house as you can to shorten the length of pipe, which might freeze, and to simplify priming or draining the line. Accessibility means putting a removable cover on the well, rather than burying it under the lawn (wells only have problems in the middle of winter, when the ground is frozen hard). The logic of those two things taken together is not to build the house atop the well with the idea that it will all be warm and accessible in the basement. The pipe that must occasionally be pulled out of the well may be 30 feet long or more and is very stiff. If you have a basement with a 30-foot ceiling, go ahead and put the well down there. Otherwise, put it close to the house, with a removable cover and an insulated pipe.

Properly set up, the modern pump and pressure tank take very little maintenance. The most common problem seems to be frost. Box in the exterior line with four inches of insulating foam, and bury the thing as deeply as the lie of the land allows. Place the pump and pressure tank inside the house where they're easy to reach when things go wrong.

Pressure problems – too little or too much – are easily fixed. The pump has a little covered box on the side that contains a pressure switch. Take off the cover and look for the two settings: stiff springs with screw adjustments. One turns the pump on when pressure in the system gets too low, the other turns the pump off when the pressure is high enough. Leave the pump plugged in, and turn on a tap. Watch the pressure gauge fall and note the level at which the pump turns on, then note the pressure at which it turns itself off again. Adjust the two screws up or down until the pressure limits are suitable.

The first sign of trouble is often the sound of the pump kicking in when no one is at the taps. First, check for dripping faucets and replace worn washers . . . or yell at the last person in the bathroom. If the taps aren't dripping, chances are there is some small leak in the system. Check all accessible pipes and joints for moisture. If the inside pipes aren't leaking, look for a leak at the well.

Take two pairs of mitts (this only happens in January), and remove the well cover (weren't we clever to cover the well with something more manageable than frozen lawn?). Loosen the nuts and remove the sealed well cap, then pull out the long pipe that goes down the well (aren't you glad you're not doing this in the basement?). At the bottom end of the well pipe, you should find a "foot valve," a thing that stops the water in the pipe from running back into the well. Foot valves fail from corrosion or from a buildup of the mineral sludge that is the plumbing equivalent of cholesterol. Replace the foot valve, and try the system again. If the pump continues to tell you there's a leak someplace, examine the well pipe itself at the point where it enters the water. The uneven pulse of pressure when the pump turns on can be enough to cause a hairline crack there. You can't see it easily, because it opens only when the pump starts and the pipe flexes.

Why two pairs of mitts? Because the first pair will freeze to the pipe when you haul it out of the well. If the water has a woolly taste, ask the previous owner about pump problems.

WHAT GOES IN MUST GO OUT

Getting water into the house may be simpler than getting it out. The standard solution for water in the basement is the sump pump, a contrivance that looks like a carnival ride for mice (and may indeed serve that purpose when you're not looking). It stands in the water, sucking up through its base and spewing out through a flexible plastic hose that you've had the foresight to fit through the basement window in a general downhill direction (if you spew it out the uphill side, it may leak back into the house). The two balls that hang from the top of the pump tell it when to turn on and off. The upper ball is a float. When the water reaches the float, it lifts a switch and the pump turns on. The lower ball is a weight. When the water drops below that level, the unsupported weight of the ball turns the pump off.

The usual routine is to stand the pump in a hole cut in the basement floor. Adjust the upper ball at the top of the hole, and the pump will turn on automatically just before your hole runneth over. The only maintenance is making sure that the flotsam doesn't plug the inlet holes around the base.

If the city house didn't have a sump pump, it's because the city house had drains buried outside the foundation and a drain in the basement floor.

Those drains, connected to a big-city storm sewer, carried the rain away before it could seep through to the rec-room floor. More modern country houses emulate the city way in every respect but the storm sewer (and perhaps the floor drain). The key element is the perimeter drain (usually a four-inch perforated pipe) buried outside the foundation about as deep as the basement floor. It should have an outlet that runs downhill to a dry well or a ditch. Properly installed, the perimeter drain should be maintenance-free. All you have to do is trace the outlet from house to ditch and remember never to plant trees along that line – the roots will clog the drain.

That's the easy part. The tricky bit is the potentially more offensive effluent. The true delineation between town and country is the appearance of the ubiquitous backyard mounds and green spots that mark the septic tanks. Not to worry. The backyard tank does much the same job that the best of the big-city treatment plants do. It's just a little closer to home. Time and friendly bacteria do most of the work. Briefly (and without the sniggers, please), the system consists of a large tank and a leach bed of perforated pipes. The sewage flows into the tank. The solids sink to the bottom, and the liquids run out into the leach bed. Bacteria in the tank break down the solids into a somewhat more benign sludge. Problems arise if the bacteria die. Then the buildup of solids fills the tank and clogs the leach bed.

The bacteria die from user negligence. Everybody in the household has to realize that the toilet is not a chemical garbage disposal. It is not the place to flush away paint thinners, bleach and other things fatal to friendly bacteria. Goldfish and baby alligators are fine: contrary to myth, they won't grow into monsters under the lawn. The greater danger is household chemicals. I know, I know, sometimes it seems that there is no safe place to dispose of the darned things. That's a problem for the whole society, and it's just as dangerous to flush some of those things into the city sewer. But we're talking about a society of one here, where you have to take personal and total responsibility for what you put under your lawn. The effects of dumping just a little bit of vile stuff can't be hidden among millions of other miscreants, as it can in the city. The effects are sitting out there killing your bacteria. And if the bacteria are not there doing what they're supposed to do, the solids build up quickly, until you pull the handle and flush the lot onto the bathroom floor. Not nice. If anything, we can say that here, at least, cause and effect, ecological crime and consequence, are neatly and justly linked.

Sooner or later, no matter how contented you keep your microbial labour corps, the system may fill up with sludge. That's when you call in the local septic-pumping service. Don't be embarrassed. It's like any other bodily function that everybody has and nobody discusses. The more discreet firms let the road grime cover the company logo so that it looks like an ordinary fuel truck.

The important thing is to know exactly where the septic tank is and where the clean-out access is. When the truck arrives, the driver won't be pleased to find that in the five years since the tank was last pumped, some city folks have bought the place and built a swimming pool between the driveway and the clean-out hole.

ALTERNATIVES

The septic tank is a workable solution. It does as good a job as most city treatment plants – and a far better job than those cities, like Montreal, which don't bother with treatment but pump raw sewage straight into the public waterways. The septic tank works, and it is only a minor inconvenience to have it pumped occasionally. Nevertheless, we've spent an inordinate part of the past 15 years experimenting with the alternatives.

We started the search for alternatives because of three, admittedly personal, objections to the usual septic solution.

The first was the rock. The soil was too shallow to take tank and leach bed without trucking in dirt to cover it.

The second objection was the matter of using water to flush. When you use water in a rural system, the pump turns on. Between the flush upstairs and the pump below, there is little hope for either discretion or a quiet night's sleep as the family make their nocturnal visits.

Finally, all that flushing requires plumbing. Plumbing needs occasional repairs, occasionally urgent repairs. And the more urgent the need, the more likely it is to be a weekend, when the plumbers have all turned the business over to their answering machines.

This is the place, perhaps, for a word on the link between self-reliance and country living. There is a myth abroad that rural people may be more self-reliant because of some atavistic link with a pioneer past or something learned at farmer/father's knee. That's frog spit. Rural people are more self-reliant because they have to be. In the country, it is very much farther to the repair shop, the repairman isn't in, and no matter what's wrong, he'll have to send away for parts. So rural homeowners spend five minutes learning to solder a pipe or replace a washer because it's faster than waiting five days to have the plumber do it. Or they join the neighbourhood network of bartered skills. Doug is handy with a chain saw, Caroline knows wiring, Richard can put the plumbing back together (given enough electrical tape), Greg has chains if you get stuck in the mud, and so on. Not being naturally proficient, I have to think ahead and look for things like plumbing that looks after itself.

The classic country answer was the outhouse. Not such a bad idea, if you think about it. I had never thought about it until the day Pop Clow rebelled at the annual family barbecue. "There is absolutely nothing dumber," he proclaimed, "than wanting to eat in the yard and shit in the house." He refused to do either, on sanitary grounds, and lived to be 99.

He had me convinced, and so I resurrected our old privy: moved it over a freshly dug pit, cleaned it up, fitted a comfortable city seat with lid, even provided a can of sawdust for the sensitive. It had everything but a chrome-plated handle and the whoosh of water to make visitors feel at home. Still they persisted in wanting to eat in the yard, et cetera.

We experimented with a series of portable pots and finally settled on what amounts to an indoor privy: a two-seater composting toilet with separate hatch for organic kitchen wastes. Pop Clow would roll in his grave, but there it sits, taking up what was supposed to be the laundry room, with a car-sized fibreglass tank full of hungry bacteria. The odd thing is that it works. Odours exit the rooftop vent. The harvest from the nether end looks like wet peat moss and smells like good garden soil. The roses love it. In 10 years of heavy use, we've yet to call a plumber and have never been awakened by a midnight flusher. But few volunteer for the job of feeding the roses, visitors tiptoe through the flowers with unusual caution, small children balk at the thought that they might fall in, and one house sitter called the fire department when she thought the tank was going to explode.

That was before we solved the vent problem. Some city engineer had designed this system to include one of those whirling rooftop things that pretend to perpetual motion. It worked perfectly until winter. Then the moist exhaust froze to the vanes and gave the whirly a lopsided wobble that made it go "whup, whup, whup, whup, whup . . . " The very sound that a helicopter makes when it's right above your head. This sound started overhead, but connected as it was to the car-sized tank, the big bass drum of the organic band, the whup,whup,whup was an octave shy of the end of the world. Now it's amazing how you can get used to a thing like that. The distance from terror to indifference is about three cold nights and knowing that it can't be fixed until spring. We got so indifferent, we forgot to warn the house sitter that the apocalypse was all sound and no fury.

But I digress. The point is that there are many ways of dealing with necessity other than pulling the handle and trusting the city to take it all away. The usual way, the septic tank, is the simplest. But even it requires more of the homeowner's attention than the city solution.

HEAT

Keeping warm is the one necessity which best illustrates the peculiar mix of unexpected limits and new possibilities that country living presents. The economics of the thing do a flip-flop at the city limits.

If natural gas is the cheapest form of city heat, it's near the top in the country. The pipes don't reach that far, and the gas must be delivered in big steel bottles.

Electric heat is no bargain either. Rural dwellers pay more per kilowatt-hour. The power company's excuse is that low population density means higher line-maintenance costs. That excuse might turn out to be so much donkey doodle if someone were to mention that digging up Yonge Street to fix a wire would certainly cost more than removing a fallen branch from a rural line. But that's another story. The fact is that rural people pay more to heat electrically.

In the country, cheap heat comes from wood. Even villagers and small-town folks burn wood. Bought split, delivered and stacked, it's cheaper than the alternatives in any place blessed with trees. Few, however, buy it that way. Those who don't have their own trees buy logs in bulk or cut "on shares," exchanging their labour for wood.

The art and science of burning wood has filled whole books. The beginner might best concentrate on avoiding a few basic errors: neglecting the chimney, choosing a stove too big for the space and drying wood in basement or garage.

Dealers refer to wood stoves as "appliances," suggesting the convenience of a toaster that merely has to be plugged into the wall to make it work. It's easy to miss the fact that the chimney is part of the system too. That's where much of the expense, maintenance and danger lies. That's what one Ontario woman forgot when she bought her first wood burner. She laid the fire, lit the kindling and filled the living room with smoke. Then she realized that her new appliance probably should have been connected to a chimney first.

Few first timers are as careless as that. But connecting a new wood stove to an existing chimney without a careful inspection isn't much of an improvement on not connecting at all. It is vital that the chimney be clean and sound. Some jurisdictions require a permit and/or a fire inspection before the stove is installed. Your building inspector will know what inspections are required. If the law doesn't require it, your own sense of self-preservation should. Even a sound chimney should be checked and cleaned regularly during the heating season. It isn't a difficult job (the stove dealer can supply brushes and rods), but it is an essential one. If the mess puts you off, there are commercial chimney-cleaning services everywhere.

Part of the fire inspection (where it's required) is to check for safe clearances between the chimney and any combustible materials as well as clearances around the stove itself. If an inspector doesn't check clearances, check them yourself. The safe limits should be marked on any stove you buy.

The second mistake is believing that bigger must be better. Bigger is, indeed, warmer. And warmer might be just what we want on the coldest nights of the year. Unfortunately, the stove will also be burning on the not-so-cold nights. On those nights, you will have to leave the windows open or cool off the stove by closing the air inlets, choking the fire by withholding oxygen. The open-window policy wastes wood. The closed-stove policy saves wood (that's the basis of the "airtight" claims), but without oxygen, the wood doesn't burn completely. The fire is hot enough to drive out volatile gases but not hot enough to burn them. Instead, the gases go up the chimney and condense as creosote, a black, tarry goo that will ignite in the chimney when it's least convenient. That's where chimney fires come from. Better to have a stove that's a little too small for the house than to have one a little too big. The safe way is to have smaller, hotter fires and thicker socks.

Dry firewood is the first defence against chimney fires and the one area where the new wood burner is least likely to get good advice. Because the seller said so or because it happened to be cheaper, you end up with wood that isn't ready for the fire. If you burn it "green," it will put far more creosote into the chimney. What to do? People stay dry by staying indoors, so you put the wood in the basement, in the garage or under plastic. Right? Wrong. The moisture is already in the wood. The object is to get the moisture out. Protecting the woodpile from rain is a noble sentiment, but it won't dry out with the existing moisture trapped in place. That's akin to putting the wet laundry in a plastic bag – it won't get any drier in there. Firewood has to be exposed to air. That's why it is split – not to make the pieces smaller but to expose the long, split sides to the air. Stack the wood in single rows, at right angles to the usual breeze. Stack it as high as you like and as long as you like, but only one row wide. Turn the bark sides up to help shed the rain, or put a cover atop the pile. Just don't let the cover droop down over the sides of the pile where it would impede the breeze going through. One summer in an open pile is better than years in a garage or closed woodshed.

GARBAGE

The one question that urbanites may forget to ask when considering a country neighbourhood is, What happens to the garbage? It isn't a trivial question, nor are the answers consistent enough to be able to guess. The consumer economy might be regulated, monopolized and planned to the last plastic doodad, but dealing with the debris at the other end remains a hodgepodge of local solutions.

Inside the city, it can be as simple as knowing where the garbage chute is and remembering not to empty the ashtray there. The urbanite is assured that at least his mess will be hauled away. Hauled away where is not often his concern. It's a safe bet that the city garbage won't end up inside the city limits; it will be hauled away to the countryside where it offends fewer voters. That's where you and I come in.

Living near a dump isn't nice. Even if the smell, the gulls and the rats are too far away to offend, the poisoning of the water table with whatever it is they're burying there will sooner or later come out of your taps.

Check the neighbourhood before you move in. Ask the town clerk where the dump is or where the next one is planned. Ask if there is a garbage-pickup service and, if so, where it goes. Ask what residents do with the larger garbage: the fridges, shingles and derelict cars that the garbage man won't accept. Is there an unofficial dumping spot? What about nearby townships?

When it comes to garbage, the first simple enquiry is rarely enough. One rural Ontario township boasts an almost-metro garbage plan: weekly pickup at the end of the lane, a hardworking crew that takes just about anything that can be lifted and a road crew that cleans any scattered mess that coons and dogs might make. Sounds ideal, but the next-door township saves its tax dollars by having no garbage service at all. On Sunday night, a stream of furtive cars comes across the township line, leaving bags of foreign garbage for the Monday-morning pickup. The more responsible of them leave their bags at the end of somebody's lane, where they stand a chance of being seen and hauled away. The Visigoths toss for the ditch.

The patchwork of service prevails nearly everywhere. In rural parts of the United States, garbage has been privatized. You have to pay an entrepreneur by the bag to take it away. Kenneth Howard copes by burning and composting, flattening his tins and crushing glass to minimize the bag count. Others cope by tossing the lot into the nearest creek.

At the other extreme, many communities sponsor separation and recycling facilities and "spring cleanup days," when the larger junk is collected.

Whatever the official system might be, you can ease the burden a bit with some at-home sorting out. We keep one bag for burnables and another for plastic and glass. Anything organic goes to the compost pile if the chickens and pigs won't have it.

A compost pile, for the uninitiated, can be an odourless, pest-free way to feed the garden (and cut down on the garbage). Layer the kitchen vegetable scraps with garden waste, leaves, weeds, manure (if you can get it) or just about anything that will rot. Keep it damp and stirred, and the waste will be rich garden humus in a matter of weeks. If you don't have time to stir the pile, it will reach the same end but take longer. The heat of decomposition kills the weed seeds and pest eggs and tells you the pile is cooking properly.

Odourless? We kept a compost pile in a tiny urban backyard. The pile took fresh manure by the truckload and all the kitchen garbage from a nearby restaurant. The neighbours never suspected. We were close enough to hear a quiet conversation from kitchen to kitchen, but the garbage and manure never set a nostril atwitch.

Don't buy near the dump. Ask about collection services before you buy. Support recycling programmes. And recycle what you can at home. If you burn the paper and compost the scraps, the leftovers from the leftovers won't amount to much. It won't be any easier than it was in the city, and you will have to take more responsibility for your own mess. And maybe that's not such a bad idea.

WIRED WORLD

A country kilowatt is much the same as a city one – just a little bit more expensive. There are, however, two other differences that prospective exurbanites should know about.

The first is the cost of installation. If you're building a new house, check with the power company before you pick out the house site. It can get very costly to build more than a given distance away from the road or the nearest power line.

The telephone company can become equally picky about serving those who choose to live in inconvenient places. Solitude may be worth the price, but learn the price before pouring the foundation.

The second problem is the higher incidence of power failures outside the city. To be fair, trees do fall on lines, and there are more trees in the country. But the power companies also seem to be far more casual about shutting down a rural system in order to hook up a new house or to make a repair. Rural veterans always get a cynical chuckle out of those breathless urban newscasts describing a city neighbourhood without power for a couple of hours. In the country, the same blackout lasts for days or for all of Christmas week, and nobody says a word. The power company doesn't even say "sorry."

There's a little bit of rural resentment that the power company would take us for granted, and more resentment that the news media consider rural inconveniences less important than urban inconveniences. But the real reason that we exurbanites don't burn the poles and occupy the newsroom over the slight is that most of us are better prepared for the problem. With wood stoves, we don't worry about the heat going off with the power. And even if you prefer the microwave, the wood stove will do dinner in a pinch. Rural blackout veterans also keep candles and oil lamps handy.

Water is the one problem that new exurbanites might not expect. When the power goes off, so does the pump. There might be enough water left in the pipes to wash your hands or have a cup of tea, but forget about showers and flushing the toilet until the lights come back on. Some older properties will have extra wells: a dug well, barn well or cistern, perhaps. We keep a hand pump in an old well and have the water tested regularly to be sure it's safe to drink. It's always there when the power fails. If you don't have an extra well, an ordinary rain barrel under the downspout will provide at least enough water to flush the toilets in a blackout.

It is possible to do without commercial utilities for longer periods. And we have done just that – for years at a stretch – in the interest of peace or economy. Never for convenience, however. For convenience, we eventually return to the ordinary.

We gave up on the outdoor solar shower when visitors persisted in arriving unannounced. Faced with a choice between moving the shower indoors or getting a telephone so visitors might give more warning, we moved the shower indoors.

The telephone caused other problems. Three things had persuaded us to do without: years of working at the end of a phone and resenting the intrusion, an estimate of $3,000 to install a 10-party line and the knowledge that half of those lines would ring on our phone, always in the middle of the night.

We managed without. Friends wrote letters to keep in touch. Salesmen stayed away. Others were less understanding. One Montreal contact eventually reached me at the "office" number (a phone booth three miles away). He refused to believe it was a phone booth. He couldn't understand why no one had answered the phone earlier.

"Where is this so-called phone booth?" he sneered.

"In front of The Store."

"What store?"

"The Store. That's what it says on the sign. That's what it's always been called. That's what it's called in the phone book: The Store."

At that point in the conversation, a stranger rode up to The Store on a horse (I'm not making this up). He dismounted and went in. The horse, bored and all alone by the gas pump, spied a potential apple bearer in the phone booth. He came over to check me out. I closed the door. He pushed at it with his muzzle. I braced. He bumped harder.

"What's that noise?" asked the man from Montreal.

"That's a horse."

"Oh yeah. Your horse, I suppose."

"No," I assured him, "I've never seen this horse before in my life."

"A strange, unattached . . . horse . . . that . . . just . . . happens . . . to be . . . running . . . around . . . in your . . . office." He stopped between the words, as if he were trying to write it down.

"No . . . (Thump) . . . he's trying to . . . (Thump) . . . push his way into the . . . (Thump) . . . phone booth . . . Hello? Hello?"

I never heard from him again.

SOCIAL ADJUSTMENTS

▼▼▼▼▼

Are newcomers to small society destined to wait a generation before they can really belong? Us and them? A wave on the road, a word about the weather, a guarded acceptance that is the social equivalent of safe sex?

Maybe. It depends on the place, and it depends on the newcomer. Most of all, it depends on whether the newcomer can adjust to the subtle differences between rural and urban society. Understand first that small society is not a tidy pyramid, arranged in a vertical hierarchy of class or wealth. Money helps, but social acceptance depends as much on how long you've lived in a place, what you do for a living, your urban ways and even your religious and political colours.

Religion doesn't have to become a problem or a point of division unless you flaunt yours or, worse, disparage someone else's. The secret is not to go recruiting door to door. For the most part, indifference rules. There are Catholics who live happily among the Plymouth Brethren and Baha'is on the library board. St. Theresa's Catholic Church, up the Sissiboo in Southville, has 18 names on its memorial plaque – 16 of them are Cromwells!

Party politics, like religion, has lost its fire. On the other hand, the small "p" politics of local issues still has the power to divide any community, and the unwary newcomer might easily fall through the rift. Small towns fight over whether to approve abortions in the local hospital, whether to build a shopping mall, where to put the dump. They fight over herbicides in the park and skateboards on the sidewalks.

Sound familiar? Here's the difference: In the city, such issues are often fought in the abstract; even if you're personally involved, the fight doesn't spill over to spoil your place in the community. In smaller places, there's nothing abstract about such issues. It's personal. And any bad feelings outlast the cause. Those who hunt and trap will not welcome those who post "no hunting" signs almost as soon as the curtains are hung. Farmers who have counted on selling off a few building lots for their retirement will not welcome planning studies and petitions organized in an attempt to stop development. The posters and petitioners are not merely taking abstract stands on the wider issues of animal rights and farmland preservation; they are spoiling the fun and profit of their neighbours, and that kind of interference won't easily be forgotten.

Occupation is a familiar social measure, but again, there are differences worth paying attention to in smaller places. Here, the industrial base matters – though only to a degree. In agricultural areas, the biggest ranchers or richest farmers predominate. In mining towns, the mine manager sits fairly high on the social scale. But in general, small-town society has the pinnacle of its pyramid removed. Branch plants of large industries have local managers, but they are subordinate to less visible bosses in some distant head office. The local manager receives respect but is not accorded a lot of status. Small-town status still seems to devolve on those with old money and on those with classic professions that remain independent and carry with them the weight of tradition: the doctor, dentist, newspaper publisher, owner of a local business.

Length of residence is the first dividing line between us and them, between new arrivals and those who already belong. The problem is at its worst in the smallest, most isolated, most static communities. There, the distance between us and them might be measured in generations. Your grandchildren may eventually be accepted as locals, but you haven't got a prayer of ever being anything but "the city people who bought the old Edwards place . . . paid too much, you know . . . must have money . . . put in two new bathrooms and one of those hot-tub things where everybody gets in together . . . can you imagine? Mrs. Edwards will be turning in her grave."

Of all the divisive behaviours in small society, few are more ruinous than displaying or espousing urban ways.

Even the lines between old and new residents can be softened if the newcomers make the effort to adjust themselves to the local mould. The small-town equivalent of original sin, however, is to flaunt the big-city airs in the face of local ways. Leaving the kids in city schools because the local ones aren't good enough will be social suicide. Jogging for exercise past neighbours who are aching to take a break is acceptable, as long as you don't stop to lecture them on aerobic benefits. Having wildflowers in the garden is almost acceptable – planting them there will put you on the lunatic list, and ordering wildflower seeds from the catalogue will guarantee you peace and quiet for 20 years to come.

Small societies are neither simple nor homogeneous. The trick to a happy move is biding your time, neither flaunting your differences nor trying too hard to mimic local manners and ways. Use that time to survey the local society, see how it works, and then decide just where you would like to fit in.

There are some simple ways to test the social waters. First, make an effort to look for visible differences within the community: Can you see different races, different ways of dressing, unusual shops . . . or does everybody look alike? The mere presence of differences doesn't guarantee that everybody gets along, but it does increase the odds that you'll be able to fit in with one group or another, even if you didn't happen to be born there.

Second, spend a few hours in the library reading back issues of the local paper. Small-town weeklies are prone to boosterism and papering over cracks in the social fabric, but they will give you some idea of what's been going on and how the sides on any issue form. Read the letters to the editor to see who's complaining about what. Read the "coming events" column and the entertainment page to see how the locals spend their time. Find out how the latest development or building project was received.

Finally, spend a little time with someone who knows the town. It could be a business contact, a barber or somebody on the school board. When the ice is broken, slip in a few questions about the community. Who are the local business leaders? How long have they been here? (The newer the leaders, the better your chances of fitting in quickly.) Ask about the local oddballs – whom should you be on the lookout for? Then ask what makes the oddballs odd. Their views? Their attire? Their behaviour? Their religion? Are they any odder than you might appear to be in an unguarded moment?

All other things being equal, you'll be welcomed to the small society with the same enthusiasm, or lack of it, that the society shows for other new arrivals. You'll face the same divisions and the same tolerance of your own differences.

In general, the more fluid societies – those which have had to cope with some recent growth or change – are more accepting than the static places that don't see strangers often. Societies accustomed to change are more likely to see your eccentricities as spice in the life of the community. They can still be small and cheap and pleasant and have all the charm of other small places, but if the place has seen strangers other than you, your entry will be easier.

Okay, you've checked out the town, and it's a tolerant, interesting, fluid kind of place that doesn't object to strangers. You've checked yourself out and are assured that you're not too odd to fit into a smaller society. Now how, exactly, does it work? Who visits whom, and how does the society function? As you might have guessed, it won't work the way it worked in the city.

NEIGHBOURHOOD

The biggest difference stems from the fact that "the neighbourhood" plays a different role in smaller places. The physical neighbourhood – the block, the street, the cluster of houses – is less homogeneous than a city neighbourhood. In the city, planners and real estate prices act in tandem to ensure that residential neighbourhoods are bland amalgams of the same kind of people. There's no law that says doctors have to live in one neighbourhood and mechanics in another. No law but the law of economics. The doctors are the only ones who can afford to live in certain neighbourhoods. So there just happen to be lots of fellow doctors on the block for socializing and friendship. The neighbourhood, in the city, can be a very social place.

In a small town or village, the doctor is more likely to be living beside the garage mechanic or the music teacher. The other doctors might be scattered over a 20-mile radius. If the doctor wants to unwind after a hard day at the table, maybe have a drink, tell pathogen jokes and talk about tax shelters, she probably goes to visit fellow doctors. That's exactly how it works in the city, except that in the city, the doctor goes next door. In the village, she gets in the car to go visiting.

Lest that seem like a backward step, consider the advantages of this more heterogeneous neighbourhood.

First of all, rural neighbourhoods are more like mutual-benefit societies than social places. Rural residents can't just hang around the backyard on the weekend, barbecuing steaks and visiting over the hedge. There's work to be done: gardening, fixing, getting in the wood. This is where the neighbourhood mutual-aid society and informal microeconomy come into play. When the doctor can't get her car started in the morning, she doesn't call the garage. She goes next door to the mechanic's house and borrows a set of jumper cables. And when the mechanic goes away for the weekend, he asks the doctor to feed the dog. That doesn't make them bosom buddies, and they may never trade dinner-party invitations, but they come to rely on one another to fill needs that city people assign to institutions.

It would be pressing the point too far to call it a higher rural ethic. It may just be that in the country, the institutional answers to life's little problems (the boarding kennel and the 24-hour garage) are unavailable, too distant or too expensive. You use the neighbours instead.

Nor is it a flawless system. Some neighbours take more than they give, and the system adjusts itself to that. But by and large, that's how it works. The rural neighbourhood is less a society of friends, with equal incomes and interests, and more of a mutual-aid society.

A learned professor tells me that nonurban places are not as friendly as myth would make them out to be. There isn't much visiting back and forth between neighbours, he says. And he makes an unflattering comparison to village societies in places like Bangladesh where, according to the professor, villagers are far more prone to spend social time visiting around the neighbourhood.

That's probably true. And it's also true that the Third World village is a far more homogeneous place than the kind of rural neighbourhood we're talking about here. Economics and a more limited range of job opportunities keep poor villagers in a common economic state. And they can't get in the car to go off and make friends in a wider selection of places. They have little choice but to socialize with their neighbours. They're as stuck as the doctors in the suburb, who live with a lot of others in the same homogenized economic state and are too isolated by urban traffic to visit more distant friends.

In terms of social patterns, the Bangladesh village may have more in common with the suburban doctors and lawyers than it has with a mobile North American rural community. Neighbours here do have social intercourse – don't get me wrong – it's just that it doesn't always have the intensity of tightly woven lives that the myth of the village suggests. It isn't the society of equals that might be seen in Westmount or Rosedale or Bangladesh. It isn't the isolated dependency that drew pioneer villages together. And it isn't the web of extended, intermarried families that it was before the automobile allowed the youngsters to date farther away from home.

All those things remain to a degree: there is some equality in living in common geography, there is some isolation that draws rural neighbours more closely together, and there are large families that dominate some communities. But none of those conditions suffice to fill the social lives of newcomers to the country. Indeed, our lives would be poorer if they depended on homogeneity, isolation and intermarriage for social fulfillment.

As a newcomer to a country place, you won't be part of what's left of the old extended families. You can visit them, befriend them, help them and count on them. But you shouldn't count on them for Christmas dinner. You can never be part of that family circle.

Your social life will depend on keeping old friends that you'll see less often and on making new friends who will almost certainly be more widely scattered than most city friends. It would be too much to expect that you'll have lots of boon companions just over the backyard fence. If you play your cards right, you will have lots of helpful neighbours just over the backyard fence but no guarantees of intimacy.

Here's how it worked for us. Our newfound neighbour turned up on the day we raised the walls and at firewood time. He pulled us out of ditches and spent hours leaning on trucks, explaining who is related to whom, where the deer feed, what the newcomers paid for their house, when the ice goes out of the lake and how to harness a pig. In return, we gave him hay from the fields, lent him our livestock box, chased his cattle and introduced him to home-brew beer.

The marrow of the thing was struck, however, on the cool spring morning when I got a hurried call to come help at the birthing barn, a swayback relic that's closer to our place than his. A little black and white cow was all bunged up with her first and far-too-big calf. Doc Stewart was there to cut through the flank, but they needed hands to catch the calf as it slithered through the long incision and hands to hold the bovine innards in until he could sew her up again. We struggled to keep the swaying mother on her feet while Doc and the obstetric conscripts worked elbow-deep in her belly. The calf came out like an avalanche of water balloons, all bagged and quivering. We pulled the little guy out of the sack and pulled the guck out of his mouth to start him bawling. I felt like being sick and singing simultaneously. I did neither. I did what everybody else was doing, which was to wipe off the mess with handfuls of hay, pat the cow and pretend that it was all in a day's work and time to get back to the chores. Then, later, I did what everybody else did too, which was to sneak back to the barn every afternoon to see how mother and son were getting on.

Probably some thanks were said, but no mention made of quid pro quo. It would have been unthinkable. And unthinkable to refuse the request. The remarkable thing, in urban eyes, is that neighbours might be close enough to share in a thing as intimate as birth and yet never share a meal or exchange a Christmas card. The mutual-aid society that is the rural neighbourhood is at once more intimate and more distant than any city suburb.

By contrast, we once moved into a city house and were greeted with flowers and a bottle of wine. A most gracious welcome from the next-door neighbours. They were very nice people, just like us. We had similar incomes, similar educations, the same employer, same number of children and much polite conversation. We shared a driveway and most vital statistics but very little else. For privacy's sake, each family spoke softly when using the back gardens and pretended that the neighbours were not also conversing 15 feet away. It was intimate in the sense that we lived within a lazy reach of one another and yet distant in the sense that good manners and the need for privacy raised invisible barriers.

We exchanged food and drink and Christmas cards. We also kept a reserve that would have precluded sharing a birth. We would have called in professional help and not presumed upon the neighbours. Fred once asked to borrow a cup of cognac, and that's the most intimate demand they ever made on us. Liz and I were talking about that the other day. We were sitting on the front verandah listening for the mailman. We can hear him coming from about half a mile away. We can stroll down to the mailbox and get there about the same time he does. It isn't that he has a noisy muffler; it's just that even the tiny sounds carry clearly when there's nothing to compete but bird song and the breeze.

"Funny how the breeze makes a different sound in different trees," she observed. "Funnier still how much I notice things like that now. The limit of my senses has moved . . . way out there . . . " and with a wide sweep of the arm, she included the whole green circle, clear to the horizon.

"I don't think I could ever . . . " (she thought for a moment and then hunched her shoulders and scrunched up her face) " . . . ever condense myself enough to live in the city again. Remember how we used to sit in the back garden in the city and pretend that the neighbours weren't just on the other side of the flowers? As if there were a thick glass wall all around and we had to focus on our little patch of grass so everything beyond would cease to exist?"

That's what intimate social distance means. Physically and socially, our country neighbours are far more distant than that. If the professor is right, that's normal. If the professor is right, that's more distant than Bangladesh. We don't share the drive, the flowerbed border or family conversations. We don't have the same employer or the same vital statistics. Nobody greeted us with flowers and wine. They came to help instead. That's a different kind of distance and a different kind of intimacy.

Urbanites whose rural experience is limited to antique auctions and asking for directions are easily impressed with rural helpfulness, and they jump too easily to the conclusion that people are unusually friendly in the country. If those same people then move to the country, they may be shocked to find that full social acceptance doesn't come quite so quickly. It takes generations to be accepted, lament those who have tried to fit in and failed.

In fact, both sides of that contradiction are partly true, and neither is absolutely true. In fact, rural society is as Byzantine as any other. There are layers and classes and factions and vast differences between one township and another. Any generalization will be at least half wrong in half of the places.

The best that can be said is that newcomers might be advised to hold a little in reserve, waiting to see the lie of the local land before diving headfirst into the shallow end of the social pool. Social success outside the city depends as much on avoiding mistakes as it does on doing the right thing.

THE LIE OF THE LAND

Stewart is a big-city lawyer with enough social savvy to mix anywhere he chooses. He calls cabinet ministers by their first names and conducts his business all around the world. The one place he will never succeed, however, is at the sprawling lakeside place he owns in the country. It won't be for lack of trying. Stewart married a local girl. He remembers people at Christmas. He doesn't talk down. He deals with local tradesmen. Money and power aside, he is still a very nice man. But he has one social handicap that he will never be able to overcome in his lifetime—he has a city man's view of property.

Here's what happened: Long before anybody now alive can remember, someone cut a track through the hardwood bush. It might have been to serve the one old ramshackle house on the shore. It might have been to skirt the swamp that lies behind it. Whatever. In recent years, the power-company crews have kept it open to reach some isolated sections of line. It isn't much—just a twisting path through the trees, barely enough to accommodate hikers, skiers, snowmobiles and maybe very determined four-wheel-drive vehicles. The fact that it connects at either end with a long network of woodsy seasonal roads makes it a handy—almost essential—link for all the locals who enjoy the outdoors.

When Stewart bought the lakeshore, the deed reached up into the high hardwoods and swallowed a significant part of the track. No problem there. Somebody else owned it before him. But Stewart committed the unforgivable faux pas of assuming that because he had paid for it, it was his. They should have forgiven him because he is, after all, a lawyer and therefore couldn't have known any better. But Stewart took the deed seriously and took objection to strangers crossing "his" land without permission. Being from a big city, he didn't realize that the trespassers weren't strangers at all. They knew exactly who they were and where the track had always taken them.

Things got complicated when thieves made off with tools and a pump and Stewart assumed that the disputed track was the getaway route. If he had asked, anybody could have told him that a sensible thief would come across the lake on the ice and not risk getting stuck on a dirt track through the bush. But Stewart didn't ask. He put a big steel gate across the track where it crossed his paper boundary. And "No Trespassing" signs. It didn't occur to him that, in the local view, he himself might be seen as the trespasser. The locals went around the gate. Stewart built a fence so that they couldn't go around. The locals opened the gate. Stewart added a vault-sized padlock. The locals lifted the gate from its hinges and swung it open the other way. At this writing, that's where it sits: the gate at the side of the track, the padlock still in place, the opening marked with a winter's worth of traffic. Stewart will arrive from the city in a month or so. Everybody will be friendly and polite. Nobody will use the trail while Stewart's in residence. He'll add a bigger lock or weld the hinges shut. Then he'll leave again, and the usual winter traffic will resume.

The lesson is that there is a certain order fixed on the rural landscape that has nothing to do with ownership. It covers more than presumed right of passage. There are the places where longtime residents swim, fish, hunt, pick wild berries, picnic and just plain trespass. Newly arrived urbanites can fight those traditions, but not even the richest lawyer in the district can win without paying a social penalty.

Better to ask before you buy. Asking "What do the locals use this for?" is a more useful question than "Where do the boundaries lie?"

We've backed into the old urban view of property rights more than once, to our great regret. And only once have we managed to restore the historic equilibrium. That was over the deer hunt.

It's easy to laugh at the deer hunt. At times, it seems to have as much to do with camaraderie, alcohol, dogs, trucks, male bonding and getting out of the house for a week as it does with any atavistic urge to gather food. Laughter is too facile, however. A series of hunting accidents and near misses moved us once to post 100 acres against the hunters.

174

It wasn't any softhearted effort to save the deer that moved us, though we regularly thrill at the sight of a doe and fawn stealing apples from the orchard or a big buck sailing over a fence. (Those sights alone should have taught us a lesson about boundaries and property rights.) No, we were more concerned about two small children who wandered through the woods at will and about Josephine, the matriarch of all milk goats. Josephine, you see, was a tawny brown with a white underbelly and a snow-white patch beneath her tail. She stole apples and sailed over fences in stiff-legged bounds that were the very image of a deer . . . if you missed the swinging udder underneath.

So we put up signs for Josephine's sake and for the children's sake. What we forgot, however, was that very few deer can read. They continued sailing over the fences as they had always done. And in hunting season, the dogs came right behind. They couldn't read either. And where the deer and the dogs went, so went the hunters, even the ones who could read.

Some of the hunters stopped to ask if they could follow the chase across the land (as they had always done), and we declined. We explained about the goat and the children, which sparked protests that the hunters could tell the difference. And at any rate, less considerate hunting parties were crossing the land and not bothering to stop and ask or read the signs.

In time, wind and rain removed the signs, Josephine dried up, and the children took up tennis and bikes instead of wandering through the woods. We would still rather watch the deer than see them shot, but our real defences were gone.

When the hunters came back to ask once more if they could cross the land, we agreed. Better they should hunt with permission than without. We explained again why we had refused and explained why we were now relenting.

Nevertheless, in a last-ditch effort to subvert the inevitable, I set out to cut firewood on the first day of hunting season. At best, the sound of the chain saw might confuse the dogs. At worst, the noise might deter the hunt around the woods in question. Three things happened.

First, I met a neighbour on my way to the woods. He wasn't hunting. Never does. Like me, he'd rather watch the deer. We talked about the fine buck we had both seen crossing the road shortly before. We knew where the wild apple trees were and knew exactly where the buck was headed. Then a party of hunters stopped on the tree-lined gravel road. "Seen any deer?"

"Nope," says the neighbour, leaning on the truck. "Haven't seen any deer all fall. Must be the apples all dried up."

We exchanged some words on the weather, the truck drove off, and the neighbour and I went back to talking about the buck. My neighbour wasn't being unfriendly to the hunters. He knew them all. Had known them all for 40 years. One was a sort of a cousin.

The second thing that happened was that I got my truck stuck belly-deep in the mud in the middle of my own woods. I threw out the big load of firewood and still couldn't move the beast. I dug and jacked and levered and swore until the day was nearly gone. I had just about given up when a gang of hunters appeared – the same hunters who had ignored the signs in past years. Pushing the half-buried truck proved futile, so half the gang went off to get their four-wheel drive parked on the distant road. The tow rope broke, flinging one of the hunters off the truck and into the mud. The rest went off again to get a chain. Eventually, truck, chain and four wet hunters dragged the old Ford and its load of firewood to the road. By then, it was dark and there was no hope of catching the deer or the dogs they had been following.

I said, "Thanks."

They said, "No problem." Nothing at all was said about sawing wood on the opening day of deer season or about the landowner's permission.

The third thing took place a few days later. The hunters came back, asked me if I had got all my wood in and then gave me a big roast of venison. "We had a pretty good hunt," they said. "Thought you might like some."

That same night, the other hunters stopped – the ones who had always asked permission to cross the land and had been so long denied. "Thanks," they said. "We finally got our deer a couple of miles away. Thought you might like a piece."

And the buck? The big prize who had spent the day in the wild apple trees? Saw him a few days later, walking out of the woods behind the house. The neighbour's way worked much better than signs.

BIG-EYED CREATURES

The one defence of the deer that would not have worked would have been the claim that they're too cute to kill. That softhearted, often-misguided view of the natural world is a stake in the heart of urban-rural relations. It's the social equivalent of moving to Westmount and putting a tractor-tire planter on the lawn. And, no, that doesn't mean that your new country neighbours are beer-swilling, dog-kicking despoilers of the planet. Some are. Most aren't. Most have pets of their own. They have dogs that sleep on the bed, cats they talk to and caesarean calves that get more than their share of coddling. They have a goat named Grover who waits in the wheelbarrow for rides. There was a pug that lived for weeks in one hunter's pocket. Country people can be just as silly about animals as anyone else. They must, at the same time, be very realistic about the obligations and responsibilities that animals entail. They know, among other things, where meat comes from and what that means. They know that that feisty little caesarean calf will become some urbanite's McWhopper. And harvesting "government cattle" (one local term for deer) doesn't take a harder heart than killing the McWhopper calf.

Country people know that animals don't always benefit from human comforts. The urban transplant sees a herd of snow-dusted cattle on a bitter winter day and thinks how cruel it is to keep animals outdoors in such conditions. The farmer knows, however, that it would be far crueller to keep the steers in the barn, where dampness would quickly make them sick. Don't assume that the farmer is cruel; he might just know what he's doing.

The farmer knows that his cow is smart enough to prefer the green grass beside the road to whatever's left in the field and stupid enough to lurch in front of any oncoming car. He also knows that the cow cannot be persuaded back into the field with baby talk and a handful of grass. Harsh shouts and a whack on the flank aren't cruel if that will move the cow onto the path of social responsibility.

Urban transplants who dream of small-scale farming quickly learn that you can't raise a farm animal like a pet, or you'll never be able to eat it. And if you coddle it, you'll look like a fool. That's why my farmer neighbours were just a little discreet about coming back later to check on our caesarean. And that's why the vet almost throttled the Trilbys over Doris.

The Trilbys bought a small farm, just big enough for a couple of large dogs, a horse and a cow. They didn't have children, so they substituted animals. The cow, Doris, was intended to be part of the self-sufficiency plan, but no milk came and Doris got crankier by the day. A neighbour kindly explained that Doris would have to be bred before she could be milked. It might even improve her mood. That seemed reasonable, even to the Trilbys. But these were back-to-nature types, and there wouldn't be any of this artificial stuff for them. Doris would have to be done nature's way. Unfortunately, her would-be suitor lived six miles away. Since ramps and swaying trucks seemed too cruel an artifice, Doris would have to walk to her rendezvous. So Julie trained Doris to a leash and "walked" her there. Doris didn't take to the leash and long walks with the same enthusiasm as the dogs, but that's another story.

The upshot was that Doris came home in the family way, and Julie converted the barn into a maternity ward. She fattened the already generous ration and wore a rut from the house to the barn with her "checks," which expanded into nearly all-night vigils as Doris came closer to "term," as Julie put it. She called in the vet for prenatal checks until he was heartily sick of the sight of fat old Doris, not to mention Julie.

Finally, on one nightly vigil, Julie heard a pained, rumbly, gratey sound that seemed to be death and despair. It came again and again from somewhere deep within. Julie raised the lantern in the half-dark stall and looked for a mangled head to appear. Whatever it was was deeper than that, and it wasn't coming out. Doris kept her eyes closed tight and stayed, sprawling fatly on the floor. It was three o'clock in the morning, but Julie figured that time was of the essence and that the vet would have to be there for whatever trouble was coming. It took a while to convince him that he really had to get out of bed to help Doris with her awful labour. But he did. He arrived in his pyjamas and overcoat and stood, disbelieving, at the byre door.

"What the hell's the matter?" he snapped. Julie was nearly in tears. "I don't know," she snapped back. "Just listen to that horrible groaning."

"Groaning?" demanded Doc. "That cow's snoring. What I meant was, what the hell's the matter with you?"

The next time Doc saw Doris, she was dead – not from the eventual birth but from rabies. Julie and husband and dogs and horse all had to come in for rabies treatments. Shortly afterwards, they left the farm, unreconciled to nature's strange ways.

Rabies is one of several reasons that even nonhunters keep guns in the country. Foxes that stagger among the cows have to be shot. Period. In many places, a fox or a skunk that appears boldly, acting unafraid, is not a cute extra from a Disney set. It is a potentially dangerous animal, and shooting it is not an act of cruelty but an unpleasant necessity that might have saved Doris. Rabies isn't the only pest. Groundhogs eat the garden. Raccoons will strip a corn patch bare or scatter garbage everywhere. Porcupines destroy trees and can make a whimpering mess of the dog. Beavers cut and flood acres of forest without a thought for the waste they leave to rot. Talk about despoilers of the planet!

Sometimes a pest must be destroyed. If you take the baby-seal route, you won't be popular in the neighbourhood. Don't even consider the moral dodge of trapping nuisance animals to release them somewhere else "in the wild." If the critters have grown up feeding on garbage and gardens, they'll starve in the real wild or be eaten by predators they're unprepared for. And if you release the trapped pest any nearer to its former backyard habitat, you're merely dumping your nuisance on someone else. Then they will have to kill it or trap it and return it to your garden. Dumping your pests on the neighbours is extremely bad form in the rural protocol.

Some studies show that dogs are the most common country pest. Allowed to run at will, they eventually gang up and inflict themselves on the whole neighbourhood. Dogs chasing livestock can and will be shot without an ounce of sympathy for the dog owner who thought Rover would enjoy life more on the loose in the country, where there's lots of room to run. Dogs also scatter garbage and kill deer with as much callous disregard for the rules as any human poacher. Unless you want to live as a hermit, keep your dog at home.

The same can be said for all your animals. Goats would rather eat apple trees than grass, especially if the grass is theirs and the apple trees belong to the neighbour. Hens are most content when out of the pen, scratching bugs and weeds, the picture of pastoral peace. But, unlike children, they'd rather have Brussels sprouts than weeds. And if the Brussels sprouts are growing next door, the hens could care less. The people next door do care, however, and fences are de rigueur for social harmony. In many places, the fence means more than neighbourly peace. It's the law. Line-fence laws spell out just what your obligations are. When in doubt, check with the local municipal office. Some rural jurisdictions even appoint part-time fence inspectors to settle disputes over who is obliged to fix what.

THE RULES

Adjusting to new social norms can be tough on the transplanted urbanite, if only because the important rules are so subtle that they're hard to see. Your new neighbours may speak the same language, enjoy the same entertainments and, in general, live lives that are almost indistinguishable from the familiar suburban milieu. Even in the most isolated backwater, the locals mow lawns, barbecue on hot weekends, wear Adidas and watch television. Social success, or even tolerance, depends on the newcomer's ability to learn the new rules before making mistakes that will mark him or her forever an outsider. Each place is different, but here are a few rules that are common to most of the places I know:

1. Ask for advice – don't offer it. Longtime rural people carry around a few myths of their own. One is the vision of urbanites as know-it-all consultants, ready to tell the less fortunate how to live. Transplanted urbanites too quick with their opinions may well be right, but they damn themselves with the stereotype. It's like that one American tourist in a thousand who actually makes the mistake of saying, "Back in the States, we do it the other way." All the locals look at one another and whisper, "See? What did I tell you about Americans?" There is no more endearing compliment you can pay to your new neighbours than to ask for their advice. What's the best time to plant potatoes? Where's the best place to take the kids swimming? Who are the best candidates for township council? You don't have to take the advice. You win the points just for asking.

2. Offer help – don't ask for it. Asking for help is acceptable once your place in the new society is well established. But asking – as a stranger – poses some dilemmas: If you offer to pay, you label yourself an outsider, not part of the mutual-aid society that is the rural community. If you don't offer to pay, you risk being labelled a cheapskate as well as an outsider. If you ask the helper to make that decision for you (as in What do I owe you for your trouble?), then you'll force him to expose himself as either a grasper or a patsy. Even if he is one of those, he'll resent having to make the choice.

In the beginning, when you need help, buy it from a local business, an establishment that can tell you exactly how much you owe for their trouble and can tell you without embarrassment or resentment. You might know perfectly well that your next-door neighbour could fix your lawn mower faster and better than the engine repair shop five miles down the road. But you're not supposed to ask him yet. Ask instead if he would recommend a good repair shop in the area.

Offer help whenever it's needed and with whatever skills you have. Better still, offer labour and forget the skills. Skill comes uncomfortably close to advice. Offering is easy. Just wait until you see a neighbour struggling – a car in the mud, one man with a two-man load, a wandering cow or whatever – then simply get out and do it.

Once the work is done, you might introduce yourself, but only if you need to know your neighbour's name. He already knows yours. He also knows what kind of person you are. No money will be offered for your labour, nor much effusive thanks. But when you next need help, it will be there, without the need to ask.

3. Get out of the house. The surveys say that there is little difference in the way urbanites and rural people spend their time. They spend about the same amount of time working (a little more in the city), doing chores around the house (a little more in the country), and about the same number of hours each week on leisure activities. What the numbers don't winnow out is the slightly different way in which rural people socialize. If you move to a country neighbourhood and wait for an invitation to drinks and dinner, you may well starve.

Small communities have more public social functions than private ones. Fairs, church suppers and community picnics are occasions for mixing and visiting. The only invitation issued may be the hand-drawn poster in the grocery-store window.

Ayr puts on a pig roast every summer. It started as an ad hoc fund-raiser for junior sports, became a contest for whole-hog chefs and is now an annual tug-of-war, sit-on-the-grass, swim-in-the-old-Nith-River party. The 1,350 villagers turn out with such enthusiasm that the last head count put 6,000 people at the party.

The place to meet the neighbours is in the park, at the rink, at the post office, store, fund-raiser or any public event. Go to local auctions – they're social events. Go to stags, showers and wedding receptions, even if you haven't been invited to the ceremony itself; the before-and-after parties are wider community affairs, often seen as fund-raisers for the couple. Your presence will be noted, as will your absence. Go to wakes and funerals, even if you didn't know the deceased very well. It's a mark of respect for the family.

4. Finally, be yourself. We've suggested that the urban transplant has to make a few adjustments. But those are adjustments to social habits, not adjustments to the self. Nobody expects you to wear gingham, play country music and spit just because you moved to the country. Your neighbours would be offended if you did. It would look as if you were making fun of them – or making fun of the way that Hollywood imagined that country people lived 50 years ago. If you would rather play the harpsichord and wear a hula skirt, then do it. Just don't offer advice, ask for help or sit at home like a hermit.

EPILOGUE

One of the enduring pillars of social intercourse is the small-world story: how you happened upon an old school chum in a distant place or learned that the stranger beside you was a long-lost cousin. The fascination in unlikely meetings hangs on the wonder at the eerie tides that move us. "What brings you to this place?" is more than idle chat. It's the step before the scary metaphysics of "Where do we go from here?"

The last time I saw Sandy C. was over a pool table in a basement in London, England. He was waiting for an assignment in Africa. That was a dozen years ago. So naturally, when my new neighbour this year turned out to be a Swiss German from Mozambique, I asked him if he knew Sandy C. As a matter of fact, he did. They met in Maputo. Small world.

Such unlikely threads should be even less likely in small rural places, places that are so readily dismissed as isolated, unchanging places. Cosmopolitan paths cross in cities, don't they?

Americans used to say that if you stood by the lions on the steps of the New York Public Library long enough, everyone you ever knew would eventually walk by. The English held a similar conceit, substituting Nelson's column as the locus of all paths.

But the small-world stories wouldn't be so engaging if they all took place on the steps of the New York Public Library. That's like my chickens all meeting in the same nest every day. It's not only probable, it's predictable. What makes the small world interesting is the opposite element of *im*probability. All roads do not lead to Wawa or Camden East or Rideau Ferry. What odd forces, then, must be at work to bring diverse people to the little places?

What brings a Swiss mechanic from Mozambique? A young family from the Yukon? An elegant matron from Prussia, whose three grown children have chosen to settle in three separate countries? A family from India that, in its search for smaller places, moved first to London, England, then to Manchester and finally here? An inventor? An ex-Member of Parliament? Czechs and Finns? A professional athlete and a poet? A general? A baker? An undertaker? Even a farmer or two? What long roads they've travelled. What stories they tell.

And yet, I know how easy it would be to pass this tiny community in the blink of an eye. It looks for all the world like a thousand other backwater places: a store (The Store), a telephone booth and a bridge where, in summer, youths dive 30 feet to deep waters below. How easy it would be to see only the surface and pass by the rest on cruise control. How easy to dismiss it all as one more sleepy, isolated, unchanging place. Not at all like the meeting of diversity that is thought to live solely inside the city limits.

Small world, eh?

APPENDIX

▼▼▼▼▼

LOOKING AROUND

Deciding where to live is a complicated business. The most important parts of the question are the personal considerations, with which no book can help:

How far should we move from old friends and family? What kind of community suits us? Small? Big? Back-slappy? Reserved?

What kind of terrain do we like? Seashore? Forest? Wide-open skies?

Then there are the economic questions that must also take a personal turn. Can we get jobs there? is a question that can't be answered without first asking, What kinds of work are we capable of? and How much money do we need?

The least important questions may be those which are the same for everybody. These are the things that can be reduced to impersonal numbers and drawn on a map. These belong at the back of a book: Where is the weather best, the air cleanest, the gardens most sublime?

Even these questions must still be seen through a personal filter. Geographers can tell you where it's warm and where it's not, but you have to decide which you like. Nor do gardens have any absolute scale of fecundity. If we moved far enough south, we could grow bananas – but would have to give up on apples. A personal choice.

Then there's the risk that our experience in one place clouds our judgement of other places. When we lived in a warmer place, we loathed winter. The snow was a grey, slushy mess that puddled at curbs, soaked our feet and followed us into houses. Sixty miles from the city and a few degrees colder turned winter into a favourite season. Now the winter landscape stays white and clean, frozen hard enough to walk outside in bedroom slippers without getting wet.

Keep all those provisos in mind as you make judgements about the places where the living might be better or cheaper.

LAND-PRICE DISTRIBUTION

Land prices vary according to a lot of local criteria (see "Keeping the Links"). But the general levers that jack up prices are population density and competing use.

Population density is obvious. When more people want to live in the same space, they bid the prices up. Consider this brief list of land prices and densities:

City	People/square mile	Land cost/square foot
New York	64,992	$3,430
Chicago	13,180	1,190
Los Angeles	6,384	790
Dallas	2,715	290

Competing commercial uses drive up land prices even if there are no residential pressures on the land. In most cases, it's not desirable residential land anyway. Not unless you like living beside a strip mine or a freeway exit. The occasional exception is agricultural use. If the land is valued for agriculture, you'll pay a premium to live there. You may also be removing good food land from production. The best rural bargains are for uncleared land, rocky land and marginal or abandoned farms.

GARDENING

Don't look for good garden soil on an agricultural map. Gardens are little pockets of soil that will take some special treatment regardless of what the rest of the country is like. You can improve the quality of the soil more easily than you can improve on the rainfall, sunshine, slope, frost and wind conditions. Get those factors right in your land search and worry about tilth and fertility later.

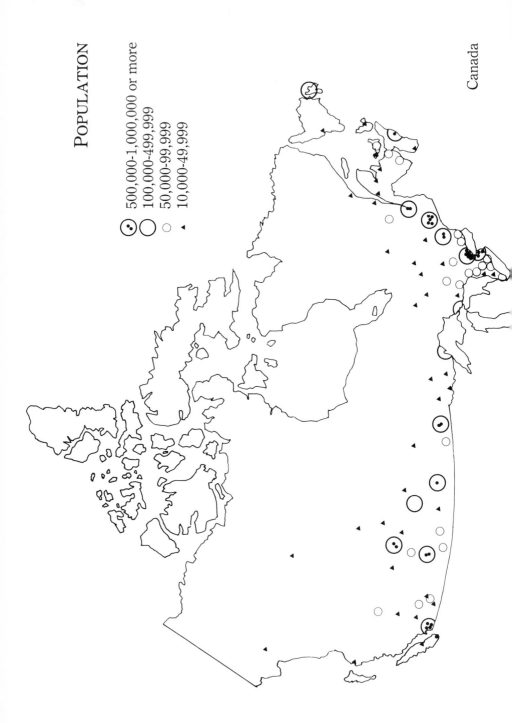

POPULATION

500,000-1,000,000 or more
100,000-499,999
50,000-99,999
10,000-49,999

Canada

POPULATION
U.S.

1,000,000 or more
250,000-999,999
50,000-249,999
10,000-49,999

MEAN ANNUAL GROWING DEGREE-DAYS

Obtained by accumulating differences between 5 °C and the
mean daily temperature for every day of the year when the mean
temperature is above 5 °C. Each degree Celsius above 5 °C is
considered as one degree-day.

Canada

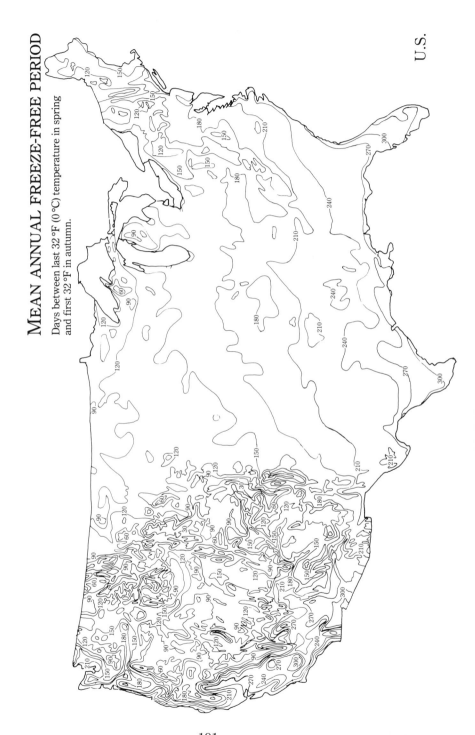

MEAN ANNUAL FREEZE-FREE PERIOD

Days between last 32 °F (0 °C) temperature in spring and first 32 °F in autumn.

U.S.

POLLUTION

Clean air is closely related to population distribution. The bigger the city, the dirtier the air. Winds and local climates can move it away more quickly or trap it in place. And industrial sources can make "hot spots" that won't show up on a big map. These maps show a broad view, but a local check of weather and sources is still advisable.

It is possible to map the distribution of acid rain from its industrial and auto sources, but its effects may be tempered where natural limestone formations can neutralize the acidity. Look for local limestone if you're worried about acid rain.

Clean water is critical if, like most rural people, you plan to rely on a well for domestic supply. There are some steps you can take to clean up home water (see "Domestic Science"), but it's always better to find a clean source. Generally, the farther removed from the city and the higher the ground, the cleaner we expect the water to be. There is, however, a vital exception: farm pesticides are starting to show up in the water table.

The other big water danger is underground leaching from old industrial waste sites. These aren't well mapped, and the land buyer has little choice but to do some judicious checking through local environmental agencies.

WEATHER

If your dream is to move where the weather's better, consider your criteria carefully. Lots more sunshine sounds great, but ozone depletion and increased ultraviolet penetration may make it less desirable. More winter sun may be healthier than summer rays.

Similarly, a location with the fewest rainy days sounds ideal for outings, but all that picnic weather might ruin any chance of success in the garden.

MEAN NUMBER OF DAYS
WITH SMOKE/HAZE

Canada

TOTAL DAYS OF HIGH
AIR-POLLUTION POTENTIAL

U.S.

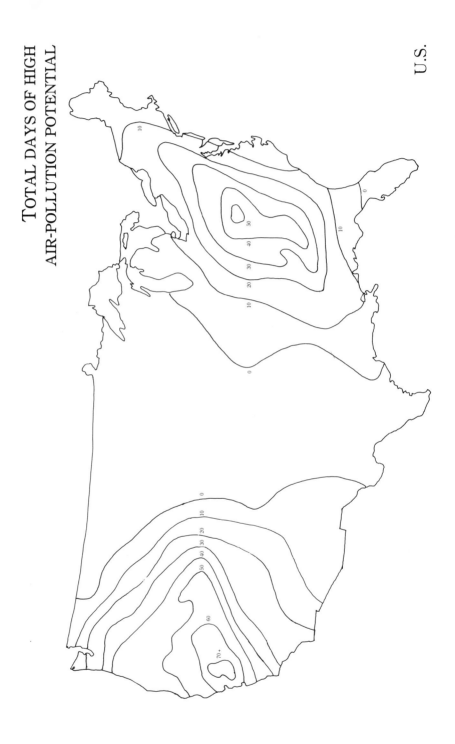

STAKING A CLAIM

Buying rural property is not much different from buying city property, with two important exceptions. First is the fact that weather and seasonal differences have a relatively greater impact in the country. Secondly, the legal fine points have – in the past – been a little more informal outside the city. Both of those differences can bring unpleasant surprises for the unwary.

First, the seasons. When you look at a city property, you look at structure and street and things that don't change very much from season to season. Little things, like the quality of the shade, might not be quite as expected. But by and large, what you see in any one month is what you get in 12.

That's not necessarily so in the country. The October idyll might be plagued with mosquitoes from May to Labour Day. That lovely, shady summer lane might be under water all spring. A serene winter site might be spoiled by the summer onslaught of cottagers. George and Ida Morrow moved from the middle of the continent to the coast. They invested all their dreams in a house that overlooked the sea. That whole first summer was an endless holiday of swimming, clamming, shelling, wading and basking in the salty breeze. Then they spent a winter freezing, as the breeze turned to gales that drove damp, icy drafts through every crack. They moved again.

The lesson is to take the time, if possible, to watch a country property through four full seasons before you commit your future to it.

The informal approach to the legalities does not imply dishonesty. Things get fuzzy with time. When the property line runs from the big rock to the leaning oak to the edge of the little creek, it can shift a bit over the years. Survey stakes disappear, and tradition takes over. That works fine for a few generations, but when somebody severs a lot and the surveyors run the line anew, don't be surprised if the line isn't exactly where the salesman thought it was. Pay for the survey before you buy.

Water rights, mineral rights, rights-of-way and easements are based on historic complexities that never come up – until somebody tries to exercise the rights. Then, it can come as a nasty surprise. Can you dam the stream across the farm? Can your neighbour dam it upstream and leave you dry? Have past owners sold off the mineral rights? Who has rights to build a road across the land? Where do the easements lie? Those are lawyer questions. Hire one.

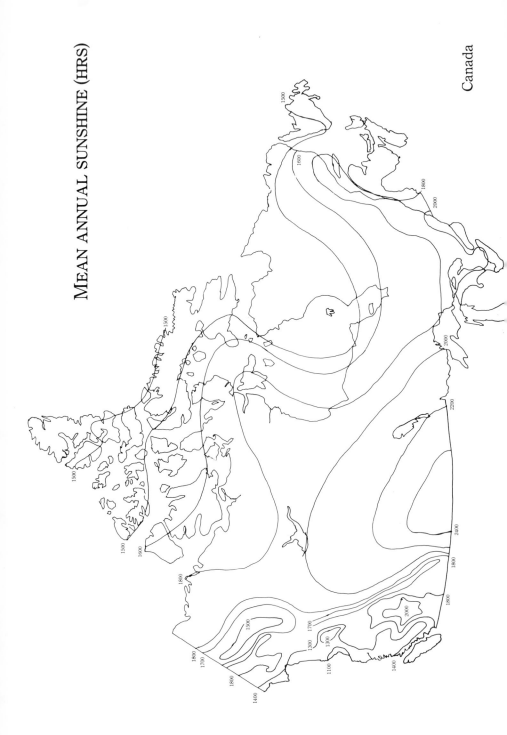

2400

2800

2800

2400

2800

2800

2800

3200

2800

2800

3600

3800

4000

4000

3200

2800

2400

2000

2800

2400

2000

1800

2000

2400

2800

MEAN ANNUAL PRECIPITATION (MM)

Canada

MEAN ANNUAL PRECIPITATION (CM)

U.S.

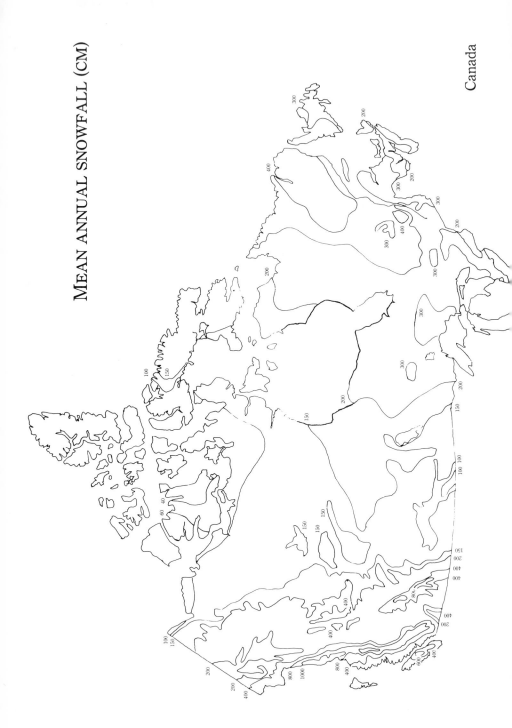

U.S.

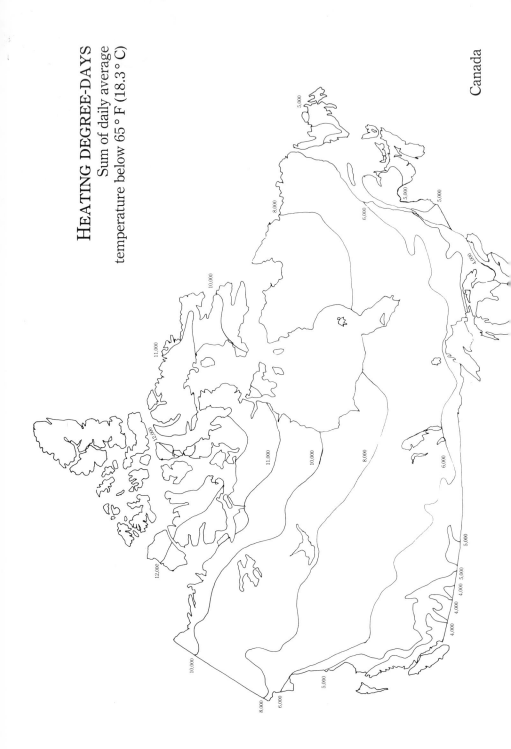

HEATING DEGREE-DAYS
Sum of daily average
temperature below 65 ° F (18.3 ° C)

Canada

Heating Degree-Days
Sum of daily average temperature below 18°C

U.S.

RECENT INCREASES IN PRICES OF HOMES
IN EIGHT NORTH AMERICAN CITIES

Note that the following prices should not be used to make comparisons between Canadian and U.S. conditions, since statistics were compiled using different methods. Data for the four Canadian cities come from Royal LePage's surveys of Canadian housing prices. Prices shown are average ones; they are based on both data and opinions as to fair market value supplied by Royal LePage personnel in those cities. Data for the four U.S. cities come from the National Real Estate Association in Washington, D.C. Prices shown are median ones; they are based on sales of single-family dwellings and townhouses but not condominiums.

TORONTO (NORTH TORONTO)

Detached bungalow   Executive detached two-storey

Year	Price	Price change, one year	% change, one year	Year	Price	Price change, one year	% change, one year
1980	$105,000	–	–	1980	N/A	N/A	N/A
1981	$135,000	+$30,000	+28.57	1981	$225,000	–	–
1982	$110,000	–$25,000	–18.52	1982	$190,000	–$35,000	–15.56
1983	$110,000	NIL	NIL	1983	$195,000	+$5,000	+2.63
1984	$116,000	+$6,000	+5.45	1984	$214,000	+$19,000	+9.74
1985	$121,500	+$5,500	+4.74	1985	$230,000	+$16,000	+7.48
1986	$155,000	+$33,500	+27.57	1986	$285,000	+$55,000	+23.91
1987	$205,000	+$50,000	+32.26	1987	$365,000	+$80,000	+28.07
1988	$305,000	+$100,000	+48.78	1988	$475,000	+$110,000	+30.14

Overall percentage increase
1980-88: 190.48

Overall percentage increase
1982-88: 111.11

MONTREAL (BEACONSFIELD)

Detached bungalow   Executive detached two-storey

Year	Price	Price change, one year	% change, one year	Year	Price	Price change, one year	% change, one year
1975	$36,000	–	–	1975	$69,000	–	–
1976	$38,000	+$2,000	+5.56	1976	$70,000	+$1,000	+1.45
1977	$36,000	–$2,000	–5.26	1977	$61,500	–$8,500	–12.14
1978	$41,000	+$5,000	+13.89	1978	$68,500	+$7,000	+11.38
1979	$45,000	+$4,000	+9.76	1979	$76,500	+$8,000	+11.68
1980	$61,300	+$16,300	+36.22	1980	$104,900	+$28,400	+37.12
1981	$67,700	+$6,400	+10.44	1981	$114,200	+$9,300	+8.87
1982	$51,500	–$16,200	–23.93	1982	$89,100	–$25,100	–21.98
1983	$54,500	+$3,000	+5.83	1983	$89,000	–$100	–0.11
1984	$61,000	+$6,500	+11.93	1984	$101,000	+$12,000	+13.48
1985	$75,000	+$14,000	+22.95	1985	$126,000	+$25,000	+24.75
1986	$100,000	+$25,000	+33.33	1986	$165,000	+$39,000	+30.95
1987	$120,000	+$20,000	+20.00	1987	$200,000	+$35,000	+21.21
1988	$122,500	+$2,500	+2.08	1988	$205,000	+$5,000	+2.50

Overall percentage increase
1975-88: 240.28

Overall percentage increase
1975-88: 197.10

VANCOUVER (RICHMOND)

Detached bungalow				Executive detached two-storey			
Year	Price	Price change, one year	% change, one year	Year	Price	Price change, one year	% change, one year
1975	$57,000	–	–	1975	$80,000	–	–
1976	$60,000	+ $3,000	+ 5.26	1976	$86,000	+ $6,000	+ 7.50
1977	$63,000	+ $3,000	+ 5.00	1977	$90,000	+ $4,000	+ 4.65
1978	$66,000	+ $3,000	+ 4.76	1978	$90,000	NIL	NIL
1979	$79,000	+ $13,000	+ 19.70	1979	$118,000	+ $28,000	+ 31.11
1980	$112,000	+ $33,000	+ 41.77	1980	$185,000	+ $67,000	+ 56.78
1981	$150,000	+ $38,000	+ 33.93	1981	$230,000	+ $45,000	+ 24.32
1982	$105,000	– $45,000	– 30.00	1982	$140,000	– $90,000	– 39.13
1983	$130,000	+ $25,000	+ 23.81	1983	$175,000	+ $35,000	+ 25.00
1984	$125,000	– $5,000	– 3.85	1984	$160,000	– $15,000	– 8.57
1985	$120,000	– $5,000	– 4.00	1985	$160,000	NIL	NIL
1986	$125,000	+ $5,000	+ 4.17	1986	$165,000	+ $5,000	+ 3.13
1987	$132,000	+ $7,000	+ 5.60	1987	$185,000	+ $20,000	+ 12.12
1988	$145,000	+ $13,000	+ 9.85	1988	$225,000	+ $40,000	+ 21.62

Overall percentage increase
1975-1988: 154.39

Overall percentage increase
1975-1988: 181.25

HALIFAX (DARTMOUTH)

Detached bungalow				Executive detached two-storey			
Year	Price	Price change, one year	% change, one year	Year	Price	Price change, one year	% change, one year
1975	$43,000	–	–	1975	$67,000	–	–
1976	$48,000	+ $5,000	+ 11.63	1976	$72,000	+ $5,000	+ 7.46
1977	$52,900	+ $4,900	+ 10.21	1977	$77,500	+ $5,500	+ 7.64
1978	$54,000	+ $1,100	+ 2.08	1978	$79,500	+ $2,000	+ 2.58
1979	$60,000	+ $6,000	+ 11.11	1979	$96,000	+ $16,500	+ 20.75
1980	$63,000	+ $3,000	+ 5.00	1980	$105,500	+ $9,500	+ 9.90
1981	$71,500	+ $8,500	+ 13.49	1981	$125,000	+ $19,500	+ 18.48
1982	$75,000	+ $3,500	+ 4.90	1982	$135,000	+ $10,000	+ 8.00
1983	$82,000	+ $7,000	+ 9.33	1983	$155,000	+ $20,000	+ 14.81
1984	$85,000	+ $3,000	+ 3.66	1984	$155,000	NIL	NIL
1985	$80,000	– $5,000	– 5.88	1985	$140,000	– $15,000	– 9.68
1986	$86,400	+ $6,400	+ 8.00	1986	$144,200	+ $4,200	+ 3.00
1987	$88,000	+ $1,600	+ 1.85	1987	$145,650	+ $1,450	+ 1.01
1988	$88,000	NIL	NIL	1988	$152,000	+ $6,350	+ 4.36

Overall percentage increase
1975-88: 104.65

Overall percentage increase
1975-88: 126.87

SAN FRANCISCO

Year	Price	Price change, one year	% change, one year
1981	$121,600	–	–
1982	$124,900	+$3,300	+2.71
1983	$129,500	+$4,600	+3.68
1984	$129,900	+$400	+0.31
1985	$140,600	+$10,700	+8.24
1986	$161,200	+$20,600	+14.65
1987	$171,300	+$10,100	+6.27
3rd quarter 1988	$213,700	+$42,400	+24.75

Overall percentage increase
1981-third quarter 1988: 75.74

NEW YORK

Year	Price	Price change, one year	% change, one year
1981	$73,800	–	–
1982	$70,500	–$3,300	–4.47
1983	$88,900	+$18,400	+26.10
1984	$105,300	+$16,400	+18.45
1985	$134,000	+$28,700	+27.26
1986	$160,600	+$26,600	+19.85
1987	$183,500	+$22,900	+14.26
3rd quarter 1988	$192,600	+$9,100	+4.96

Overall percentage increase
1981-third quarter 1988: 160.98

TAMPA

Year	Price	Price change, one year	% change, one year
1979	$38,400	–	–
1980	$45,200	+$6,800	+17.71
1981	$51,900	+$6,700	+14.82
1982	$53,900	+$2,000	+3.85
1983	$55,500	+$1,600	+2.97
1984	$58,400	+$2,900	+5.23
1985	$58,400	NIL	NIL
1986	$61,100	+$2,700	+4.62
1987	$63,800	+$2,700	+4.42
3rd quarter 1988	$67,900	+$4,100	+6.43

Overall percentage increase
1979-third quarter 1988: 76.82

SALT LAKE CITY

Year	Price	Price change, one year	% change, one year
1979	$53,800	–	–
1980	$58,000	+$4,200	+7.81
1981	$62,900	+$4,900	+8.45
1982	$64,600	+$1,700	+2.70
1983	$64,300	–$300	–0.46
1984	$65,800	+$1,500	+2.33
1985	$66,700	+$900	+1.37
1986	$68,500	+$1,800	+2.70
1987	$69,400	+$900	+1.31
3rd quarter 1988	$70,000	+$600	+0.86

Overall percentage increase
1979-third quarter 1988: 30.11